(OLD TESTAMENT)

General Editor: John C. L. Gibson

LEVITICUS

LEVITICUS

G.A.F. KNIGHT

THE SAINT ANDREW PRESS
EDINBURGH

THE WESTMINSTER PRESS
PHILADELPHIA

Published by
The Saint Andrew Press
Edinburgh, Scotland
and
The Westminster Press ®
Philadelphia, Pennsylvania

Typeset in Great Britain
by Print Origination, Formby, England

Printed and Bound in the U.S.A.
by R. R. Donnelley & Sons Company, Crawfordsville, Indiana

ISBN (U.K.) 0 7152 0479 1

Library of Congress Cataloging in Publication Data

Knight, George Angus Fulton, 1909–
    Leviticus.

    (The Daily study Bible series)
    Bibliography: p.
    1. Bible. O.T. Leviticus—Commentaries.   I. Bible. O.T.
Leviticus. English. Revised standard. 1981.   II. Title. III.
Series: Daily study Bible series (Westminster Press)
BS1255.3.K56   222'.13077   81-3007
                        AACR2

ISBN (U.S.A.) 0-664-21802-4
ISBN (U.S.A.) 0-664-24569-2 (pbk.)

GENERAL PREFACE

This series of commentaries on the Old Testament, of which Dr. Knight's volume on *Leviticus* is one of the first, has been planned as a companion series to the much-acclaimed New Testament series of the late Professor William Barclay. As with that series, each volume is arranged in successive headed portions suitable for daily study. The Biblical text followed is that of the Revised Standard Version or Common Bible. Eleven contributors share the work, each being responsible for from one to three volumes. The series is issued in the hope that it will do for the Old Testament what Professor Barclay's series succeeded so splendidly in doing for the New Testament—make it come alive for the Christian believer in the twentieth century.

Its two-fold aim is the same as his. Firstly, it is intended to introduce the reader to some of the more important results and fascinating insights of modern Old Testament scholarship. Most of the contributors are already established experts in the field with many publications to their credit. Some are younger scholars who have yet to make their names but who in my judgment as General Editor are now ready to be tested. I can assure those who use these commentaries that they are in the hands of competent teachers who know what is of real consequence in their subject and are able to present it in a form that will appeal to the general public.

The primary purpose of the series, however, is *not* an academic one. Professor Barclay summed it up for his New Testament series in the words of Richard of Chichester's prayer—to enable men and women "to know Jesus Christ more clearly, to love Him more dearly, and to follow Him more nearly." In the case of the Old Testament we have to be a little more circumspect than that. The Old Testament was completed long before the time of Our Lord, and it was (as it still is) the sole Bible of the Jews, God's first people, before it became part of the Christian Bible. We must take this fact seriously.

Yet in its strangely compelling way, sometimes dimly and

sometimes directly, sometimes charmingly and sometimes embarrassingly, it holds up before us the things of Christ. It should not be forgotten that Jesus Himself was raised on this Book, that He based His whole ministry on what it says, and that He approached His death with its words on His lips. Christian men and women have in this ancient collection of Jewish writings a uniquely illuminating avenue not only into the will and purposes of God the Father, but into the mind and heart of Him who is named God's Son, who was Himself born a Jew but went on through the Cross and Resurrection to become the Saviour of the world. Read reverently and imaginatively, the Old Testament can become a living and relevant force in their everyday lives.

It is the prayer of myself and my colleagues that this series may be used by its readers and blessed by God to that end.

New College
Edinburgh

JOHN C.L. GIBSON
General Editor

CONTENTS

INTRODUCTION

A speaker in the "Desert Island Discs" radio programme was once asked which dozen books he would choose out of the sixty-six in the Bible to take with him to his desert island. With a laugh he said, "Well, I'd leave out Leviticus anyway." And that is just what many people actually do today. They leave out Leviticus, supposing that its ancient rules and regulations have nothing to say to the modern Christian. This is so, they add by way of excusing themselves, "because Christ has done away with all these old regulations and rendered them merely museum pieces."

To declare that about Leviticus, however, means that this book of the Old Testament can no longer be accepted as Holy Scripture. If so, then the phrase we use, "The Church acknowledges the Word of God, which is contained in the Scriptures of the Old and New Testaments, to be the supreme rule of faith and life", is simply not true and should not be employed today.

The regulations about sacrifice and about the priestly ceremonial worship were indeed observed meticulously in Jerusalem until the year A.D. 70. On that date the Romans sacked the ancient city, destroyed the Temple, and then forbade any surviving Jews even to live in the ruins of their ancient city. Not long after, Jerusalem was even given the pagan name of Aelia Capitolina. Thereupon the Jewish people had to make their living scattered from Babylonia in the east to Spain in the west. They grouped themselves wherever they could find refuge round the local synagogue, or built one if there was none there, for the worship of God and for the study of the Law of Moses. Yet now in their synagogue worship it was naturally no longer possible for them to fulfil many of the regulations to be found in Leviticus *literally*. Without a regular priesthood and a temple building they could no longer perform the burnt offerings, for instance, although these had been employed (at God's command!) till then. They had to spiritualize the book. What the

Jewish people did with Leviticus at that time of crisis, therefore, helps us to understand what the Christian Church also made of it in its turn. For the Church grew and spread from A.D. 70 onwards throughout the Roman Empire alongside the Jews in their *diaspora*.

THE NEW TESTAMENT QUOTES LEVITICUS

The New Testament letter to the Hebrews, written by we know not whom, comes from the period just before or just after the A.D. 70 crisis. It is able to give us a clue as to how to understand our book of Leviticus nowadays. Hebrews sees that the meaning and purpose, for example, of the regulations about the function of the High Priest in Leviticus is able to explain to us now the high priestly function of the risen Christ. In other words, while the regulations were made to fit the kind of circumstances that God's People Israel had necessarily to live through in the period B.C., the meaning and purpose of those regulations did not come to an end when the Temple ended, and when the *literal* value of the regulations was done away with. Their meaning now, as Hebrews tells us, was to be understood *theologically*. And since the word "theology" means "Word of God", or "Science of God", the theology that we meet with in the book of Leviticus must necessarily continue to apply to the life of the Church in the New Testament period, simply because it applies to the life and work of Christ himself.

We could put one aspect of the value of the book of Leviticus briefly, then, in a sentence like this: "The book of Leviticus, being part of Holy Scripture, reveals various aspects of God's atoning purpose when he used sacrifice, and the priesthood necessary to administer it, in order to accomplish his loving will for all men within the bonds of the covenant that he made with Israel."

This is what Paul means at Rom. 1:2, when he declares that the Gospel of God was promised beforehand through the prophets in the Holy Scriptures. The prophets were not only those to whom others gave the name of prophet, such as Isaiah and Jeremiah: the whole of the Pentateuch, from Genesis to Deuteronomy, was regarded even before Jesus' day as prophetic. And since the Law derived its source in Moses, it was sufficient in Jesus' day simply to declare that "Moses said . . ." to make Moses the first of the prophets. On no account should the Christian ever say that while the New Testament became Holy Scripture, the Old Testament ceased to be Holy Scripture. At least he would have to fight St. Paul on that issue!

WHERE DID LEVITICUS COME FROM?

The first five books of the Old Testament have been grouped together ever since the days of Ezra who lived around the year 400 B.C. They are known as "The Five Books of Moses", or as "The Pentateuch" (meaning "The Five Scrolls"), or simply as *Torah*. This Hebrew word means two things at the same time. It means "revelation", and it means "instruction". So this is how Israel B.C. thought of our book of Leviticus. They knew it was alive with the living Word of the living God.

The name of our book, its Hebrew name (*Wayyiqra*), is quite theological in tone, though it is merely the first word of the book, "[The Lord] *called* . . . ." Its authors thus clearly believed it to be the Word of God addressed to Israel through Moses. Moreover, it contains material deriving straight from Moses. But of course there was no temple in Moses' day. It was King Solomon who built the First Temple several centuries after Moses was dead. It was Solomon and then Solomon's successors who elaborated the worship and the priesthood at the Jerusalem Temple, though David must have begun some form of ritual even before that. Yet they did so primarily by elaborating on the *basic principles* which Moses had established in connection with the "Tent of Meeting" that we read of in the first verse of Leviticus. This Tent, about which we read in detail in Exod. 25, had been a simple affair when used in the Wilderness. The ark that it contained was merely a coffin-like box; traditionally it contained the tablets of the Ten Commandments. Moreover, it was light enough to be carried from place to place as the People of God moved step by step from Sinai to the Holy Land. In front of it a simple altar could be set up from day to day for the worship of Israel's God. Its shape and plan, Israel believed, had been revealed by God directly to the great figure of Moses. We read about this also in the book of Exodus.

For many centuries now it has been clear that Moses did not "write" Leviticus as if he had sat down and written a book. Yet Leviticus, along with Exodus, Numbers and Deuteronomy is indeed "The Law of Moses". To take an example from English history, King Alfred, around the year A.D. 800, was the first English king to produce a law code of any kind. But for two and a half centuries after his death, right up until the Norman Conquest in fact, this code of his remained in force. From month to month, however, during that period, it was added to and enlarged by the addition of individual "case" decisions. Various judges necessarily had to make decisions in situations that were always becoming more and more complicated than anything Alfred could have foreseen as civilization in England grew and developed. Yet it was still "The Law Code of Alfred" that was pushed aside when in 1066 the Normans imposed their own Continental Code of Laws. On one occasion David acted as such a judge and made a "decision." We read of it at 1 Sam. 30:24. That decision is now incorporated in Num. 31:27.

The basic elements in the "Law of Moses" come indeed from Moses. But Leviticus often deals with situations that reflect the settled life of Israel in Canaan long after Moses is dead. That is why it too contains much "case law" (expressed by such words as "If a man does so-and-so, then...") as well as what the scholar calls apodictic laws, laying down a basic principle, some of which we find in chapter 19, and which run "Thou shalt not...".

IS LEVITICUS INSPIRED?

Yet it should not be difficult to see how regulations dating from centuries later than Moses can still be headed with the words, "The Lord said to Moses..."; or how the regulations about the

Day of Atonement, for example, which were only drawn up in the 6th century B.C. could really still be "the Word of the Lord". Two points to note:

(1) The later writers of the Old Testament were sure that the Word that God had addressed to Moses was still alive and active. God himself was always alive and active, so the Law still continued to be God's Word even though the priests whom Moses had ordained were long dead.

(2) John's Gospel declares that the Word became flesh and dwelt among us in the person of Jesus Christ. Yet a couple of generations after Jesus, human beings like Peter, James, Paul and John produced material which we now call "the Word of God", and we accept their writings as inspired even though Jesus was dead when they wrote them. This New Testament parallel helps us see that in the way the Old Testament grew to completion God's Spirit was present in all stages in its development.

WHAT LIES BEHIND THE BOOK

Solomon's Temple, built about 950 B.C., was destroyed by Nebuchadnezzar, King of Babylon, in 587 B.C. The latter also took the inhabitants of Jerusalem and of the surrounding area of Judah into exile in Babylonia. Once King Cyrus of Persia had, in his turn, captured the city of Babylon in the year 539 B.C. he encouraged the "Judah-ites" (later compressed into the word "Jew") to return home and rebuild their Temple in the ruins of Jerusalem. They began their return a year later, but at first only established their homes in the old city, with a crude altar erected from the ruins of the old buildings.

It was only in 520 B.C. that, under the enthusiastic urging of Haggai and Zechariah, they got started rebuilding the Temple. Of course, at first it was not nearly so ornate as the original one had been. The opening chapters of Ezra tell us about all this, and how the new Temple was finally consecrated in 515 B.C. That five-year period must have been a very exciting time for the large body of priests who had now returned "home". There must have been many a conference on how to adapt and apply what they possessed of the ancient words of *Torah* to the routine about to be established at the building now rising in Jerusalem before their very eyes.

During the exile in Babylonia there had evidently been some faithful priests, such as our biblical prophet Ezekiel, who had pondered the *meaning* of the terrible events that Israel had now undergone. Israel had clearly been "crucified, dead and buried"—at least that is how Ezekiel understood the events. So the question now arose in Ezekiel's mind, could Israel possibly experience a "resurrection" (again in a metaphorical sense), when the dead bones might live again (chapter 37)? *Why* had Israel suffered in this way? those thoughtful exiled priests had argued and discussed. Was she indeed wicked above all other nations in the world? Had not God made covenant with Israel in the olden days with the intent that through Israel all the nations of mankind should enter into the blessedness that God had purposed for them (cf. Gen. 12:3; Isa. 45:23; 49:6)? So then how could God have allowed Jerusalem to be destroyed and his people exiled? For had not *all* humanity turned its back upon God and been "shut out of the Garden" (Gen. 3:22–24) and not just the chosen people; and was not all mankind equally and utterly and wholly evil (Gen. 6:5)? Yet were the pain and suffering that Israel had now undergone in the exile not an indication that God did indeed have an answer to the wicked-ness of man, that God could in fact still "get through" to man's hard and selfish heart with his message of love by means, somehow or other, of sacrifice and suffering? Was it not perhaps (what a scandalously new idea!) that God's own "special" people (Exod. 19:5) had in fact been called into existence in order to become that "sacrificial lamb" which God would use in his plan of universal restoration and redemption? Was it really possible that paganism could win finally against the purpose and plan of God (a situation we are faced with today) without God being able to produce a final answer to its universal threat?

ACTING OUT THEOLOGY

These and many other deep thoughts, obviously inspired by God, must have been in the minds of at least some of the priests who were now eagerly planning the ritual to be followed when the Second Temple was ready. Fortunately they possessed under God the genius to develop the theology they had inherited from the days of the First Temple, and which is to be found particularly in the books of Genesis and Deuteronomy, and then to weave it all into a programme that was meant for action and real life. It was not a mere philosophy they produced such as we find in Hinduism, which was growing up in India at the same period.

This programme has been preserved for us in the later portions of Exodus as well as in Leviticus and Numbers. The ordinary man of that period was now being invited to discover, through all the sacrificial acts that developed at the Second Temple, and in which he himself actually shared, that God had provided him and his family with a way out from the mess in which his original sin had landed both him and the whole People of God. Now it was clear that Israel need not live permanently in a permissive society.

LEVITICUS—A BOOK OF THEOLOGY

Such a fact was clearly nothing less than the work of a God of grace. And that is what Leviticus is basically concerned to say when it speaks of the mystery of grace as we see it now in the Cross of Christ.

The New Testament can tell us this because Leviticus keeps laying stress on *why* its laws should be kept, rather than giving us mere "how to do it" rules. The laws in Leviticus are there only because the Lord, the God of grace, had acted first, even before Israel had been aware of what had been happening. He had redeemed her out of the grip of Pharaoh and had given her room to breathe in a land of her own. The laws given her in Leviticus were thus the "means of grace" by the observance of which Israel could remain within the sphere of God's holy love.

And so we discover in our book the *meaning* of the atonement, the *meaning* of holiness, the *meaning* of priestly representation, the true *significance* of the Sabbath and of the various festivals, and so on. Leviticus brings us back to the central issues of the Christian faith in fact, for it leads us in the end to the Cross of Christ.

One summer I was the pastor of a united church high in the Rocky Mountains of the U.S.A. It opened up only in the short tourist season. The solid local citizens, who conducted their own services when all lay deep under snow, asked me to help them know and understand their faith. Accordingly, I intimated that I would offer a course each Thursday evening on "What we believe". But I added, "Bring your Bible". The local motels opening up for the short season were run largely by Southern Californians hoping to escape the heat. These came along in force, but carrying New Testaments only in their hands. Many of them belonged to some of the crazier sects that California breeds, "Full Gospellers", and such like. Some of them would contradict me, and quote chapter and verse for "what Paul said". So I would ask them, "Where did Paul get that idea?" and hand them a Bible, declaring, "*That* is the book of the Church". Then I added, "Look up Isaiah so and so, or Leviticus so and so, and we shall see what Paul is really saying." Those sectists scarcely knew where Leviticus was to be found. They did not like my constant referral to the Old Testament. They refused to believe their eyes when faced with the fact that 2 Tim. 3:16–17 refers to the Old Testament alone. It was beyond them to think of Leviticus as a book of theology. And so, loudly protesting, they refused to return to my course. The real reason for their dislike of my biblical interpretation was, of course, that I was making them into orthodox Christians; and they did not wish to give up their peculiar sectist views.

THE THEOLOGY OF LEVITICUS

There is only one biblical theology, and that is Old Testament theology. Leviticus has a lion's share in providing today's

Church with this orthodox theology. It tells us what is the nature of the People of God. It tells us that God is the God of redemption and of grace. It tells us that if the worshipper is sincere, then God forgives absolutely. It sets out the groundwork for the meaning of holy living. This is not something that is to do merely with the soul (that idea comes from Plato), but with the whole person, as a member of the holy people, as a member of a human family, as a sanctified whole personality. (The idea that people are merely individuals is not found in Leviticus, but in Greek philosophy again. It was John Wesley who said that there is no such thing as an individual Christian.) Rather the emphasis in Leviticus is upon the holy family, not the individual. Thus it thinks of marriage as meaning children. If a woman is unable to bear children, then that is a tragedy. Marriage is not two people "shacking up together". Marriage is the working together of a family team to the glory of God.

Leviticus emphasises that what God asks of man is to walk humbly with him, in obedience to his will. To that end the first half of Leviticus (chapters 1 to 16) makes explicit what the first clause in the Golden Rule declares—"Thou shalt love the Lord thy God . . .". The second half of Leviticus (from chapter 17 onwards) explains in detail what the second clause of the Golden Rule means—"and thy neighbour as thyself".

But what most of my Southern Californians were unwilling to face up to is the central place that *sacrifice* takes in Leviticus. They didn't like its costliness. They preferred to be uplifted by the Holy Spirit. As we read on in the book we find that we are being given (by God!) virtually a theology of the Cross. It is the Cross that the New Testament makes central to our understanding of the life and work of Jesus. That then is why Jesus summoned his followers in their turn to make the Cross central in their own lives. "If any man will come after me, let him deny himself, and take up his cross daily, and follow me."

The study of Leviticus is a most satisfying and educative process in our understanding of the faith, not just of the Old Testament, but of the Bible as a whole.

LEVITICUS

SACRIFICE IS GOD'S WILL

Leviticus 1:1–9

> The Lord called Moses, and spoke to him from the tent of meeting, saying, "Speak to the people of Israel, and say to them, When any man of you brings an offering to the Lord, you shall bring your offering of cattle from the herd or from the flock.
>
> "If his offering is a burnt offering from the herd, he shall offer a male without blemish; he shall offer it at the door of the tent of meeting, that he may be accepted before the Lord; he shall lay his hand upon the head of the burnt offering, and it shall be accepted for him to make atonement for him. Then he shall kill the bull before the Lord; and Aaron's sons the priests shall present the blood, and throw the blood round about against the altar that is at the door of the tent of meeting. And he shall flay the burnt offering and cut it into pieces; and the sons of Aaron the priest shall put fire on the altar, and lay wood in order upon the fire; and Aaron's sons the priests shall lay the pieces, the head, and the fat, in order upon the wood that is on the fire upon the altar; but its entrails and its legs he shall wash with water. And the priest shall burn the whole on the altar, as a burnt offering, an offering by fire, a pleasing odour to the Lord."

The first seven chapters of Leviticus are something like a "Manual on Sacrifice" to be used by those priests who looked after the daily acts of worship that went on (1) at the Tent of Meeting in the days of the Wilderness wandering, and (2) in the Temple of Jerusalem once king David had made Jerusalem his capital city, and once his son Solomon had fulfilled David's desire to build in it a "house of God".

We begin with animal sacrifice (chapter 1). The ancient Israelites were not the only people to sacrifice animals as part of their worship. Most of the peoples who lived in the Near East sacrificed beasts to their gods. The sacrifice of animals as an act of worship is something that the human race in general imagined to be necessary. There were several reasons for this.

(i) Man feels helpless in the face of the gods. So it is only wise to placate them, and keep them sweet. For they can be quite irresponsible.

(ii) The gods can be kind at times and grant victory in war or good harvests in peace. So it is wise to say "thank you" to them.

(iii) Man should "keep in touch" with his gods, or, as we might say today, he should "keep in communion" with them for his own good.

All these motives lead to religious acts that man himself has thought up. But in Leviticus the whole issue of sacrifice is dealt with the other way round. What we find here is that God took the initiative in this matter.

(i) God called Moses and told him what to say to Israel. This way of speaking represents the Bible's conviction, as expressed by the priests of Israel over the centuries, that sacrifice was something that God himself has asked for, because sacrifice has to do with God's very own nature.

(ii) God spoke from the Tent of Meeting, and spoke to Moses only, yet through Moses to all Israel. God spoke at one particular spot and at one particular time. In the Wilderness, between Sinai and the Promised Land, God had revealed his mind and purpose to Israel alone. God did not shout down from heaven for all races and nations to hear. God spoke to Moses at that one spot where, under God's command, Moses had made ready to hear him.

This is the picture way the Bible chooses to use when it is talking theological truths. If we had been writing all this in our jargon today, we would have spoken about God's "prevenient grace" becoming known to the consciousness of Moses. But the biblical picture language is far better than our modern psychological jargon. For the biblical picture speaks to Black Africans today just as it did, in pre-scientific centuries, to the people of London who lived in Shakespeare's day.

Moses was to pass on God's Word to Israel. Israel is the new name that Jacob, the ancestor of the Hebrew people, received after he had spent a whole night wrestling *against* God's plan for his life (Gen. 32:22–32). The Word of God in

Leviticus comes to the people whom God had, by grace alone, rescued from Egypt, but who had actually sought to reject God and who had constantly despised the covenant which God had offered them. No wonder they needed to be brought back week in week out to realize their waywardness and utter dependence upon grace alone.

The first words of Leviticus express a very marvellous reality—that the living God actually revealed certain elements in his great cosmic plan of redemption to small human beings in a very small land. Pondering on this, the authors of the Aramaic version of Leviticus (Aramaic was the language of Jesus) which was read out to the worshippers in the Synagogue (after it was intoned in the original Hebrew) so that the ordinary folk could understand it the better, declare, "The Word of the Lord called to Moses". In this way the Targum, as this version was called, sought to preserve the mystery of the "liveness" of God's commands to Moses, in that they came out of the very heart of the living God.

The Hebrews were primarily an agricultural people. Their possessions were largely sheep, cattle and the various crops. That is why it was from these that they were to bring their gifts when they made a thank offering to the Lord. If it was a beast they brought, then it was to be without blemish, completely perfect, no reject like a carcase thrown aside in a slaughterhouse. "I will not offer burnt offerings unto the Lord my God which cost me nothing" (2 Sam. 24:24). This then is the principle implied here. God wants the offering to be a *Qorban* (the word we meet at Mark 7:11). It means "a gift consecrated to God", and so, in actuality, a free-will offering made in thanksgiving and gratitude to God for his goodness to man.

HOW THE OFFERINGS WERE TO BE MADE

Leviticus 1:1–9 *(cont'd)*

(i) They were to be made at that one special place which God had chosen. This was not just anywhere. In this case it was to be at the door of the Tent of Meeting. This structure together with the procedure is mentioned in Exod. 26. There the Tent is described as a very ornate and well equipped building. There is another tradition, however, about the Tent that is to be found in Exod. 33:7–11. There it is pictured, not as the *ornate* Tabernacle with its accoutrements that earlier chapters in Exodus had described, but as a simple tent, something like what the desert Arabs of the Negev (southern Israel) live in today. Moreover, in this passage God's Tent is not much different from the homely tents in which the ordinary folk in Israel ate and slept. For God was clearly sharing Israel's life and fate with her in her wilderness wanderings. The important difference between the two traditional descriptions of the Tent, however, lies in this, that at the Tent, "the Lord used to speak to Moses face to face, as a man speaks to his friend" (Exod. 33:11). The two traditions are finally interwoven at Exod. 40:34, where we are told how, when the people journeyed at God's command on a day's march and then in the evening set up their tents side by side, God did likewise. God himself marched in Israel's midst as the Divine Presence. And when they camped he was always available to speak to them through Moses. And *there* at the Tent, God was always present for Israel in a special sense. If they were to bring their offering *there* then it was not the offer*ing* but the offer*or* who would be acceptable to God. Clearly God does not want, and does not need, gifts of domestic *animals*. What he wants is grateful *people*!

(ii) The offerer was to lay his hand on the head of the beast. In this way he identified himself with it. It was as if he were saying, "When this bull goes up in smoke, it is really I who am the offering, not it". And so he was saying: "I am offering *myself* to God".

(iii) The priest was then to throw the bull's blood around the altar. Then, having cut up the carcass, he was to send the whole thing up in flames as a sacrificial offering. This kind of sacrifice was known as an *'olah,* that is, something that "went up" in smoke to God. The bowels and the leg area round the anus were naturally washed clean first of all excrement. The way that the priests explained to simple people that such an offering would be acceptable to God was to tell them that God would appreciate the smell coming from it. St. Paul makes use of this pictorial theological action at Eph. 5:2.

WHERE IS GOD TO BE FOUND?

Most people would say that God is to be found anywhere and everywhere. That is, of course, a truism. But the biblical God, about whom we learn only if we read the Bible (!), is not like that. Ever since the time when Moses discovered that God was speaking to him, not out of the bright blue sky, but out of one particular bush that was burning with fire, as if in pain (Exod. 3), we see God choosing the spot where *he* decides to meet with man. So Isa. 55:6 declares, "Seek the Lord *while* (or *where*—the Hebrew can mean both) he may be found".

That is why the Christian tells his neighbour he is much more likely to meet with God in church than on the golf course. And, of course, God's final revelation of himself is made in one man and in one man only. Paul puts it quite simply: "God was in Christ . . ." (2 Cor. 5:19).

According to Leviticus God was to be found supremely at that period in this place of sacrifice. Sacrifice means pain. The slain animal necessarily suffered at the altar. But if the offeror identified himself with the sacrificial beast, he was meant to understand that it was through suffering that he could obtain forgiveness. (This a truth which later chapters develop.) Curiously, there is no unanimity in the Old Testament about who did the slaying of the beast at the altar. At Ezek. 44:11, which is part of a blueprint for the future, it is the Levites who are meant to do it. But 2 Chr. 29:22-24 (a very late book) reports that it was the duty of the priests. However, the legislation that we find here in Leviticus prevailed in the end. Right up till A.D. 70, the date when the Romans destroyed Jerusalem and the Temple with it, and so right through the lives of both Jesus and Paul, it was the ordinary layman who was entitled to do the deed.

This is a very important issue. Later on at Lev. 17:11 we shall read, "For the life of the flesh is in the blood". Altogether the word "blood" occurs some eighty-five times in the mere twenty-seven chapters of Leviticus. Blood was regarded as peculiarly sacred to God. The shedding of this living, holy thing therefore was efficacious for the forgiveness of sins and for reconciling man to God, that is to say, it worked! We shall see what the quotation means with all its deep theological content as we proceed.

VARIOUS KINDS OF OFFERINGS

Leviticus 1:10–2:8

"If his gift for a burnt offering is from the flock, from the sheep or goats, he shall offer a male without blemish; and he shall kill it on the north side of the altar before the Lord, and Aaron's sons the priests shall throw its blood against the altar round about. And he shall cut it into pieces, with its head and its fat, and the priest shall lay them in order upon the wood that is on the fire upon the altar; but the entrails and the legs he shall wash with water. And the priest shall offer the whole, and burn it on the altar; it is a burnt offering, an offering by fire, a pleasing odour to the Lord.

"If his offering to the Lord is a burnt offering of birds, then he shall bring his offering of turtledoves or of young pigeons. And the priest shall bring it to the altar and wring off its head, and burn it on the altar; and its blood shall be drained out on the side of the altar; and he shall take away its crop with the feathers, and cast it beside the altar on the east side, in the place for ashes; he shall tear it by its wings, but shall not divide it asunder. And the priest shall burn it on the altar, upon the wood that is on the fire; it is a burnt offering, an offering by fire, a pleasing odour to the Lord.

"When any one brings a cereal offering to the Lord, his offering shall be of fine flour; he shall pour oil upon it, and put frankincense on it, and bring it to Aaron's sons the priests. And he shall take from it a handful of the fine flour and oil, with all of its frankincense; and the priest shall burn this as its memorial portion upon the altar, an offering by fire, a pleasing odour to the Lord. And what is left of the cereal offering shall be for Aaron and his sons; it is a most holy part of the offerings by fire to the Lord.

"When you bring a cereal offering baked in the oven as an offering, it shall be unleavened cakes of fine flour mixed with oil, or unleavened wafers spread with oil. And if your offering is a cereal offering baked on a griddle, it shall be of fine flour unleavened, mixed with oil; you shall break it in pieces, and pour oil on it; it is a cereal offering. And if your offering is a cereal offering cooked in a pan, it shall be made of fine flour with oil. And you shall bring the cereal offering that is made of these things to the Lord; and when it is presented to the priest, he shall bring it to the altar."

The sacrificial procedure was to be similar whether the beast chosen was a sheep or a goat, or even if it was a turtledove or a young pigeon. Always the blood had to be drained away before the flesh was burned. In the case of a bird, the bowel area was too small for the priest's fingers to squeeze clean and then wash, so he was just to throw that part of it away. Note that God does not expect ordinary Israelites to give what they could not expect to afford. Pigeons have always been plentiful around the homes of man. A man with no property therefore could always catch and offer one of these nuisances that always kept stealing his grain. Even this pest would be quite acceptable to God. Clearly it is a man's intention, his will, that matters to God, and not the monetary value of his gift.

The beast was to be a male. This is not because a female is in any sense inferior. Rather, it is because the male represents also the female and the young. In fact the male sums up the whole family. In the Old Testament it is always the family that is the unit, not the individual, and this is true, not only of man, but also of the beast that has to die not for the individual but for the family.

There is one more piece of symbolism to note. The priest is to kill the beast on the north side of the altar, "before the Lord", that is to say, as a religious act, and not like a butcher merely cutting up meat for his shop. Ps. 48:2 and Ezek. 1:4 both express the idea that while God lives in heaven—nay, "heaven and the highest heaven cannot contain him" (1 Kings 8:27)—yet when he enters Jerusalem and the holy place he does so from the north.

In this chapter 1, then, we are given a first glimpse into the mind of God on the question of sacrifice; but there is much more we are going to learn about it as we proceed.

Even after the Israelites had settled in Canaan in towns and villages, and had built up the city of Jerusalem, most people, unlike in today's Western economy, continued to live on the land. So it was that if an enemy should approach the open village, farmers and stockmen would leave their simple cottages and take refuge within the walls of the nearest city. The story in Genesis 4 about Cain and Abel shows that stock-raising and agriculture were traditionally the two main human occupations of the Near East. So those who were agriculturalists, and who grew grain rather than raised animals, had as much right and were given an equal opportunity to show their gratitude to God as had the shepherd or cowman. Right to this present day the Church everywhere has laid stress upon the grain harvest, in that congregations enjoy their annual Harvest Thanksgiving services. And this is true even of big city churches. Just to see a packet of cereals or a can of peas before our eyes in church is sufficient to remind us that it is out of the ground that God gives us our food, and that man does not create it himself.

Here verse 1 of chapter 2 speaks of a "cereal free-will offering" as something that could be offered separately. But it could also accompany an animal sacrifice, as we find happening in chapter 7. And, just like the processed food we eat today, it was the "fine flour" of the grain that was to be brought to the priest; that is to say, it was the cereal *after* it had been worked by man, at the cost of his time and human sweat. So it represented (1) what God had first created, and then (2) what man had made of God's gift.

Olive oil added to the sacrifice made it into a cake that could be handled easily, and frankincense, which was expensive, made the whole into a worthwhile "sacrifice". It was indeed a sacrifice now, and not something which cost the offeror nothing. Moreover, the offerer, who was a layman, was involved in the whole activity, for it was up to him to make all the preliminary preparations.

The phrase in verse 2, "Aaron's sons the priests" means Aaron's descendants. Aaron was Moses' brother. Right down the centuries people believed that the line of priests stemmed back to Aaron. So it was that no one could be a priest who was not descended from Aaron. In chapter 1 we saw that the offerer of an animal sacrifice laid his hands on the beast's head, and in that way identified himself with it. Here we learn that the priest could do this in place of the "layman", and on his behalf. The priest was thus a kind of go-between, representing man to God.

REMINDING GOD!

Leviticus 2:9-16

"And the priest shall take from the cereal offering its memorial portion and burn this on the altar, an offering by fire, a pleasing odour to the Lord. And what is left of the cereal offering shall be for Aaron and his sons; it is a most holy part of the offerings by fire to the Lord.

"No cereal offering which you bring to the Lord shall be made with leaven; for you shall burn no leaven nor any honey as an offering by fire to the Lord. As an offering of first fruits you may bring them to the Lord, but they shall not be offered on the altar for a pleasing odour. You shall season all your cereal offerings with salt; you shall not let the salt of the covenant with your God be lacking from your cereal offering; with all your offerings you shall offer salt.

"If you offer a cereal offering of first fruits to the Lord, you shall offer for the cereal offering of your first fruits crushed new grain from fresh ears, parched with fire. And you shall put oil upon it, and lay frankincense on it; it is a cereal offering. And the priest shall burn as its memorial portion part of the crushed grain and of the oil with all of its frankincense; it is an offering by fire to the Lord."

The part of the offering which the priest burns is called the "memorial portion" (v. 9), or, better still, the "reminder portion". When this offering goes up to God in smoke it will *remind* God of his promise to look after his loved ones, the promise he had made, as we have seen, in Exodus 19:5, when God *covenanted* to make Israel his own possession.

But the priest had to live too. For his was a full-time job. So the priest kept back part of the offering from the flames as his legitimate wages. In fact, it is from "the Word of the Lord" that this ruling was made. The priest was to receive this *most holy part* of the offering; holy, because it had now been consecrated to the holy God.

Why are leaven and honey mentioned in these verses? We remember how, at the time of the Passover, when Israel came out of Egypt, the people were forbidden to eat bread with leaven in it, (Exod. 12:8). So now the use of unleavened bread reminded Israel of God's grace and mercy. For it was entirely God's doing that, under Moses, Israel had escaped from the might of Pharaoh. What about honey? This is another food that can ferment as leaven does. Fermentation, Israel believed, reminds us of the insidious, creeping power of sin in our lives. Jesus speaks this way in Matt. 13:33. Leaven and honey could, however, be included in an offering, if it was not to be burnt completely. This represents the idea that God is glad to receive an offering even from a man riddled with sin.

As for salt, this is what Israel was to use in place of leaven. Leaven corrupts, but salt purifies. We remember how Elisha purified a spring of water with salt (2 Kings 2:20-22). So the use of salt reminded Israel to keep her part of the covenant, to keep it fresh in other words. *Salt*, said Jesus, is exactly what his followers are called to be in the world (Matt. 5:13). Too many people, who ignore the Old Testament as the key to the New Testament, suppose that "the salt of the earth" are the elite human beings of this world!

The first-fruits, of course, were eagerly awaited in the spring and so were of greater value than the later fruit or crop. After a harsh winter and a long spring the first carrot, the first sheaf of wheat was very precious indeed. But one was not therefore to devour them greedily oneself. It was these precious and valuable first-fruits, with all their nutritional value after one had eaten only stored food all winter, that went to the Lord. For no gift was good enough to express one's gratitude to God for redeeming Israel *first,* even before individuals in Israel had matured enough to realize all that God had done for them.

To this day the good folk of the Pacific Islands present their minister or priest with the first yam, the first bread-fruit, the first tomato of their crops, as a symbol of all their future offerings to the church. By so doing, they are offering their first-fruits, not just to a man, the minister or priest, but actually to the Lord, as a thank-offering for all his goodness to them.

THE PEACE OFFERING

Leviticus 3:1-17

"If a man's offering is a sacrifice of peace offering, if he offers an animal from the herd, male or female, he shall offer it without blemish before the Lord. And he shall lay his hand upon the head of his offering and kill it at the door of the tent of meeting; and Aaron's sons the priests shall throw the blood against the altar round about. And from the sacrifice of the peace offering, as an offering by fire to the Lord, he shall offer the fat covering the entrails and all the fat that is on the entrails, and the two kidneys with the fat that is on them at the loins, and the appendage of the liver which he shall take away with the kidneys. Then Aaron's sons shall burn it on the altar upon the burnt offering, which is upon the wood on the fire; it is an offering by fire, a pleasing odour to the Lord.

"If his offering for a sacrifice of peace offering to the Lord is an animal from the flock, male or female, he shall offer it without blemish. If he offers a lamb for his offering, then he shall offer it before the Lord, laying his hand upon the head of his offering and killing it before the tent of meeting; and Aaron's sons shall throw its blood against the altar round about. Then from the sacrifice of the great offering as an offering by fire to the Lord he shall offer its fat, the fat tail entire, taking it away close by the backbone, and the fat that covers the entrails, and all the fat that is on the entrails, and the two kidneys with the fat that is on them at the loins, and the appendage of the liver which he shall take away with the kidneys. And the priest shall burn it on the altar as food offered by fire to the Lord.

"If his offering is a goat, then he shall offer it before the Lord, and lay his hand upon its head, and kill it before the tent of meeting; and the sons of Aaron shall throw its blood against the altar round about. Then he shall offer from it, as his offering for an offering by fire to the Lord, the fat covering the entrails, and all the fat that is on the entrails, and the two kidneys with the fat that is on them at the loins, and the appendage of the liver which he shall take away with the kidneys. And the priest shall burn them on the altar as food offered by fire for a pleasing odour. All fat is the Lord's. It shall be a perpetual statute throughout your generations, in all your dwelling places, that you eat neither fat nor blood."

After the holocaust or burnt offering of chapter 1 and the cereal offering of chapter 2, we come to the peace offering. Everyone knows at least one Hebrew word, the word *shalom*. But we are to forget the newspaper meaning of the word as "peace" when we come across it in the Bible. The root of the word means something like *wholeness, completeness, harmoniousness.* So *a sacrifice of a peace offering* is one that aims at gaining or at least strengthening this "wholeness". That is why some scholars suggest that it refers only to the final sacrifice of a whole series of such, and so that it is meant to "complete" the series.

But there are complications. The word here occurs in the plural! Does it then refer to various separate acts by which a man hopes to obtain harmony and fellowship with God? Our word here seems to be a plural of the form *shelem* (closely related to *shalom*), and altogether to mean *keeping within a covenant of peace,* or *harmony,* or *completeness,* or *fellowship, with the Lord.* This particular sacrifice was performed, we read, in virtually the same way as those we have already looked at, and was meant to be an act of thanksgiving and praise to God.

Yet it was more also. The Covenant which God had made with Israel at Mount Sinai, now that Israel was in her promised land, was meant to be lived out in peace and harmony between both God and man, and between man and man. So this particular sacrifice evidently had a sacramental overtone to it. For one thing, it included a *zebach,* the killing of an animal. What happened with this kind of sacrifice was that part of the beast was first eaten in a sacramental meal, as we might almost call it. The sacrificer, the human person, thus got some of it. But then God got the rest. For the rest of the carcass went up to him in smoke.

The story in the Apocrypha entitled "Bel and the Dragon" is a satire on this conception of the god eating food. We can read the story in *The Oxford Annotated Apocrypha,* the Revised Standard Version, page 216. In ancient Egypt the gods were regularly fed three times a day. Deut. 32:38 tells us that the Canaanites held much the same idea about their gods. But here in Leviticus the pagan idea has been elevated to a new spiritual dimension. For here it is God's own idea, not man's, that we read about. God has given this particular sacrifice to Israel to use in order to help her along the road of life. Moreover, right through the Bible no writer seems to be ashamed of using *anthropomorphic* language. This word, *The Concise Oxford Dictionary* says, means attributing human form or personality to God. After all, there is no other way human beings can picture God. Indeed, Jesus himself finally said, "He who has seen me has seen the Father". Note what Paul says at 1 Cor. 10:18 about those who sacrifice together becoming partners at the altar.

Yet, we should note this point of *theological* importance about the "peace offering". Even this peaceful sacrament was not efficacious without a sacrifice connected with it.

FROM LEVITICUS TO ROMANS

Leviticus 3:1-17 (*cont'd*)

In verse 17 we are told that Israelite man was not to eat the fat of the beast any more than the blood. The blood, as we saw, was the very life of the sacrificial animal poured out. The fat was taboo also, however. So it came to be set apart as God's portion of the sacrificial animal. The tail, for example, which is all fat, was one of the juiciest parts of the beast and therefore was greatly prized, just like the first-fruits from one's garden or farm. So it came about that God got the best of the beast as well. Sending this part up to God meant that God and man could now eat simultaneously in communion with each other, and so in this way could maintain the fellowship of the Covenant.

What we are discovering here then is that there are several aspects of the centrality of the idea of sacrifice. In a sense we gather them all up today in the words we use in the ritual of Holy Communion. Note the words here in italics, and see how they all refer to ideas we have now handled in Leviticus: "... pleading his eternal *sacrifice,* we thy servants do set forth this *memorial* ... these *gifts* of *bread* and wine ... that they may be the *communion* of the *blood* of Christ .... Accept this our *sacrifice* of *praise* and *thanksgiving* ... *to be a reasonable, holy,* and *living sacrifice."*

The peace offering only came into use in the days of the kingdom. We find Saul, Samuel, David, Solomon and Ahaz all making use of it from time to time, e.g. 1 Sam. 11:15. But in those early days the rite was probably performed in order primarily to maintain the kingdom, and so it was more a national celebration. Again, since the contents of the book of Deuteronomy were collected and completed during that same period, the peace offering is referred to in this book also, see Deut. 27:7. Amos, however, is the only one of the great prophets to refer to it at all, in Amos 5:22. On the other hand, Ezekiel brings it into the scheme of sacrifices that he wanted to see established after the exile, once Israel should be able to return home from Babylon to their ancient city of Jerusalem and be able to rebuild the Temple. However, we should note even here that Leviticus 18 legislates for those post-exilic days of the Second Temple. By that period it is the layman who performs his own sacrifice. By that means the wondrous mystery of sacrifice, lying as it does at the heart of Israel's faith, is brought down from the theological heights to which only the learned could attain, and becomes the property of any peasant or artisan. For he learns all about it and its meaning, not by *talking* about it, but by *doing* it.

Here then we reach an important development in man's

understanding of the mind of God. The great prophets more and more raised the issue of the sacrifices that had been commanded by God himself in Leviticus and elsewhere. "What to me is the multitude of your sacrifices?" Isaiah makes God ask at Isa. 1:11. "I have had enough of burnt offerings of rams, and the fat of fed beasts . . . ." But then Isaiah turns to the intention of the human heart, and not to the outward act, supposing that the sacrifice was not performed sincerely. "Cease to do evil, learn to do good, seek justice . . ." (verse 17). Amos 5:21-24 makes this same point quite explicitly. At Amos 4:4-5 he uses a terrible piece of sarcasm. He tells of God inviting Israel to come and do two things at once: (1) multiply transgression, and (2) multiply sacrifices, to pay for their transgressions!

Thus, even though after 515 B.C., when the Temple was rebuilt and rededicated, great stress was laid upon keeping and even developing the whole sacrificial system, well before the birth of Jesus many, many Jews had come to find their spiritual home in the synagogue rather than in the temple. In the synagogue, of course, it was not possible to keep the laws of Leviticus on sacrifice *literally*. On the other hand, thoughtful, educated people were now thinking hard about the *theological* significance of sacrifice as something that the prophets and the Psalmists had been feeling after throughout the centuries before them. For example, in Ps. 51:17 we find the words, "The sacrifice acceptable to God is a broken spirit . . .". Consequently the new Christian movement that began with Jesus, found near to hand, through a study of Leviticus, all that was needed to interpret to the growing Church the meaning both of the Cross of Christ and of what it meant for the follower of Christ to present his body as a living sacrifice (Rom. 12:1).

TWO KINDS OF SIN

Leviticus 4:1-12

And the Lord said to Moses, "Say to the people of Israel, If any one sins unwittingly in any of the things which the Lord has commanded not to be done, and does any one of them, if it is the anointed priest who sins, thus bringing guilt on the people, then let him offer for the sin which he has committed a young bull without blemish to the Lord for a sin offering. He shall bring the bull to the door of the tent of meeting before the Lord, and lay his hand on the head of the bull, and kill the bull before the Lord. And the anointed priest shall take some of the blood of the bull and bring it to the tent of meeting; and the priest shall dip his finger in the blood and sprinkle part of the blood seven times before the Lord in front of the veil of the sanctuary. And the priest shall put some of the blood on the horns of the altar of fragrant incense before the Lord which is in the tent of meeting, and the rest of the blood of the bull he shall pour out at the base of the altar of burnt offering which is at the door of the tent of meeting. And all the fat of the bull of the sin offering he shall take from it, the fat that covers the entrails and all the fat that is on the entrails, and the two kidneys with the fat that is on them at the loins, and the appendage of the liver which he shall take away with the kidneys (just as these are taken from the ox of the sacrifice of the peace offerings), and the priest shall burn them upon the altar of burnt offering. But the skin of the bull and all its flesh, with its head, its legs, its entrails, and its dung, the whole bull he shall carry forth outside the camp to a clean place, where the ashes are poured out, and shall burn it on a fire of wood; where the ashes are poured out it shall be burned."

The fourth type of offering is the sin offering, dealt with in 4:1–5:13. The Law in Leviticus made a separation between deliberate sins and inadvertent sins.

(1) Deliberate sins are described most graphically in Hebrew as "sins with a high hand". You can see the poor wretch in question holding his dagger high up over his victim with deliberate intent to kill him. But the phrase "high-handed sins" covered *all* deliberate human wickednesses and not just murder. That is why even a deliberate plan to commit adultery was put in this category. Yet we are to remember that it is only because God has given human beings complete freedom of will that man does actually choose to defy his loving God.

(2) Inadvertent sins, on the other hand, God could and did forgive through the regulations we meet with here. To that end

therefore he had "told" Moses what means to use for his people to gain forgiveness. Inadvertent, in Hebrew, just means "wandering away" (like a silly sheep) from the fellowship that any member of the People of God might have with God within the bonds of the Covenant. Such sins are the kind that Paul refers to when he says, "I do not understand my own actions. For I do not do what I want, but I do the very thing I hate" (Rom. 7:15). They are the sins that arise from our human weakness and stupidity, from, in fact, "the sin which dwells within me" (Rom. 7:17). "For I do not do the good I want, but the evil I do not want is what I do" (verse 19).

As we find so often in the Old Testament, the issue is put before us in a pictorial way, like the way Jesus used when he spoke in parables. High-handed sins put the sinner right outside the area, the *place,* where God's forgiveness operated. This was because there was no sacrificial system that covered up such deliberate sins. This fact is mentioned at Lev. 7:37–38. When we reach chapter 16, however, we find God's merciful answer to this terrible situation.

We begin with the priest. For along with authority in any area of human life there must go responsibility. The priest who acts carelessly, who "couldn't care less", as we say today, hurts more than himself. He "brings guilt on the people". He shows by his lack of concern that he is not really interested in the proper performance of his calling, because he does not really *love* the common man who comes to him for guidance. Yet who is it that accuses him of doing this—his own conscience, a specially nominated committee, or what?

This chapter of Leviticus introduces us to a new word for sin. It is *hattath,* one of the many words for sin that we find in the Old Testament. It means *to miss the mark.* You pick up your bow, pull it tight, release the arrow—and miss! You have missed, not because you are wicked, but because you are stupid, silly, careless, inattentive, perhaps lazy, or more probably because you do not possess the proper *aim* in life. There was the occasion when the disciples drew Jesus' attention to a Pharisee who was saying his prayers out loud in public. "Poor fellow,"

Jesus declared, "He's hit the wrong target. The 'aim' of saying your prayers is to commune with God. But all he has 'hit' is to hear people saying about him, 'Oh, look at that holy man! Isn't he religious?'" And yet even such inadvertent sin is serious enough in God's sight to require an expensive bull as a sacrifice!

The priest's unwitting spoiling of a cultic act required the sacrifice of a young bull, one without blemish, the value of which might have amounted to as much as a year's income for many a peasant farmer. Once again the blood of the victim is emphasised. Some of it the anointed priest ("anointed" emphasises the heinousness of his offence) was to carry to that *place* where a man met with God. Then seven times over—the mysterious number that God used in creating the heavens and the earth—he flicked it in front of the curtain that hid the holy place. (See Exod. 26:31-37 for this curtain and for the rest of the equipment of the Tabernacle.) Then he had to put some of the blood on the four horns that decorated the four corners of the altar of incense (which God enjoyed smelling). (See Exod. 30:1-10 once again for this.) All the remaining blood he was to pour out of the container at the foot of the altar of burnt offering. For, of course, the blood would not have burned up if it had been poured *over* the altar. Yet, poured at the *foot* of the altar, it became associated symbolically with the meat that would burn on the altar and which would then go up in smoke.

The priest was to first put his hands on the head of the young bull, as if to say, "What happens to the bull really happens to me. The bull is now carrying my sin." Yet we are always to remember that there is no such thing as sin *per se*. There are only sinners. There was no sin on that famous island before Robinson Crusoe landed on it. Sin is what living people *do*. Thus, since "the blood is the life" (of a man), when you pour out blood, you pour out a man's life. Here the bull is the substitute for the sinning priest. So the bull's blood equals the priest's life, poured forth in an action that is meant to bring forgiveness and the favour of God.

The priest is, of course, really worthy of death. Yet God forgives the priest, provided the life poured forth should touch:

(1) the *place* of God's presence;

(2) the *curtain* that hides God's utter holiness;

(3) the *altar* that sends up the sacrifice to God above for him to eat; and

(4) mingle with the *incense* that goes right up to God's nostrils!

Sin, even inadvertent sin, is a terrible reality. For it means that the sinful man has cut himself off from fellowship with the holy, living God, and so no longer knows what God wants him to do with his life. It means even that a man's sin hurts the living God. So that is why atonement for sin must become a life and death matter, one that affects the very holiness and localized presence of the living God himself. What a deep new insight we are being given here into the meaning of sacrifice, and into the need for God's loving forgiveness and grace.

THE FORGIVENESS OF GOD (Text)

Leviticus 4:13–5:13

"If the whole congregation of Israel commits a sin unwittingly and the thing is hidden from the eyes of the assembly, and they do any one of the things which the Lord has commanded not to be done and are guilty; when the sin which they have committed becomes known, the assembly shall offer a young bull for a sin offering and bring it before the tent of meeting; and the elders of the congregation shall lay their hands upon the head of the bull before the Lord, and the bull shall be killed before the Lord. Then the anointed priest shall bring some of the blood of the bull to the tent of meeting, and the priest shall dip his finger in the blood and sprinkle it seven times before the Lord in front of the veil. And he shall put some of the blood on the horns of the altar which is in the tent of meeting before the Lord; and the rest of the blood he shall pour out at the base of the altar of burnt offering which is at the door of the tent of meeting. And all its fat he shall take from it and burn upon the altar. Thus shall he do with the bull; as he did with the bull of the sin offering, so shall he do with this; and the priest shall make atonement for them, and they shall be forgiven. And he shall carry forth the bull outside the camp, and burn it as he burned the first bull; it is the sin offering for the assembly.

"When a ruler sins, doing unwittingly any one of all the things which the Lord his God has commanded not to be done, and is guilty, if the sin which he has committed is made known to him, he shall bring as his offering a goat, a male without blemish, and shall lay his hand upon the head of the goat, and kill it in the place where they kill the burnt offering before the Lord; it is a sin offering. Then the priest shall take some of the blood of the sin offering with his finger and put it on the horns of the altar of burnt offering, and pour out the rest of its blood at the base of the altar. And all its fat he shall remove, as the fat is removed from the peace offerings, and the priest shall burn it upon the altar for a pleasing odour to the Lord; and the priest shall make atonement for him, and he shall be forgiven.

"If any one of the common people sins unwittingly in doing any one of the things which the Lord has commanded not to be done, and is guilty, when the sin which he has committed is made known to him he shall bring for his offering a goat, a female without blemish, for his sin which he has committed. And he shall lay his hand on the head of the sin offering, and kill the sin offering in the place of burnt offering. And the priest shall take some of its blood with his finger and put it on the horns of the altar of burnt offering, and pour out the rest of its blood at the base of the altar. And all its fat he shall remove, as the fat is removed from the peace offerings, and the priest shall make atonement for him, and he shall be forgiven.

"If he brings a lamb as his offering for a sin offering, he shall bring a female without blemish, and lay his hand upon the head of the sin offering, and kill it for a sin offering in the place where they kill the burnt offering. Then the priest shall take some of the blood of the sin offering with his finger and put it on the horns of the altar of burnt offering, and pour out the rest of its blood at the base of the altar. And all its fat he shall remove as the fat of the lamb is removed from the sacrifice of peace offerings, and the priest shall burn it on the altar, upon the offerings by fire to the Lord; and the priest shall make atonement for him for the sin which he has committed, and he shall be forgiven.

"If any one sins in that he hears a public adjuration to testify and though he is a witness, whether he has seen or come to know the matter, yet does not speak, he shall bear his iniquity. Or if any one touches an unclean thing, whether the carcass of an unclean beast or a carcass of unclean cattle or a carcass of unclean swarming things, and it is hidden from him, and he has become unclean, he shall be guilty. Or if he touches human uncleanness, of whatever sort the uncleanness may be with which one becomes unclean, and it is hidden from him, when he comes to know it he shall be guilty. Or if any one utters with his lips a rash oath to do evil or to do good, any sort of rash oath that men swear, and it is hidden from him, when he comes to know it he shall in any of these be guilty. When a man is guilty in any of these, he shall confess the sin he has committed, and he shall bring his guilt offering to the Lord for the sin which he has committed, a female from the flock, a lamb or goat, for a sin offering; and the priest shall make atonement for him for his sin.

"But if he cannot afford a lamb then he shall bring, as his guilt offering to the Lord for the sin which he has committed, two turtledoves or two young pigeons, one for a sin offering and the other for a burnt offering. He shall bring them to the priest who shall offer first the one for sin offering; he shall wring its head from its neck, but shall not sever it, and he shall sprinkle some of the blood of the sin offering on the side of the altar, while the rest of the blood shall be drained out at the base of the altar; it is a sin offering. Then he shall offer the second for a burnt offering according to the ordinance; and the priest shall make atonement for him for the sin which he has committed, and he shall be forgiven.

"But if he cannot afford two turtledoves or two young pigeons, then he shall bring, as his offering for the sin which he has committed, a tenth of an ephah of fine flour for a sin offering; he shall put no oil upon it, and shall put no frankincense on it, for it is a sin offering. And he shall bring it to the priest, and the priest shall take a handful of it as its memorial portion and burn this on the altar, upon the offerings by fire to the Lord; it is a sin offering. Thus the priest shall make atonement for him for the sin which he has committed in any one of these things, and he shall be forgiven. And the remainder shall be for the priest, as in the cereal offering."

THE FORGIVENESS OF GOD (Commentary)

Leviticus 4:13–5:13

But layfolk were just as culpable as the priest; so it was that, if the people sinned inadvertently, an identical ritual was required in their case, except that it was performed outside the holy place. But in verse 20 we are told that, just as sin is an *action* that a man *does,*so the priest is to perform *this* action here to make atonement for the people and thus bring them forgiveness.

The verb *to make atonement* means (a) *to make payment to wipe away or erase the guilt incurred by an offence* (that is one scholarly interpretation of this strange verb). Alternatively it can mean (b) *to cover over.* That is to say, God no longer sees the individual *as a sinner.* And so the sacrifice has actually been effective, for it makes God see the sinner as a forgiven man. The sacrifice has in a sense paid for the sinful act. Moreover, this forgiveness covers the whole family unit, husband, wife and children, for it is the family that is represented at the altar by the father.

But much more important: God, we see, has now stooped to win. He has placed in man's hands the means whereby he will forgive man's sins, if only man really wants to use these means. So finally, verse 31 actually declares that, once atonement has been made, the individual *shall be forgiven.* Notice that there are no ifs or buts, only complete assurance. For, as we shall see at Lev. 17:11, the blood has now been actually poured forth, so that we can *see* that the sacrifice has *worked.*

At Col. 1:15–20 Paul makes the claim for Christ that he is the eternal Word of God, alive, before Abraham was, just as he is alive now. Today's theologian might put it in the following way: the effective work of Christ on the Cross is in fact effective, not only forwards to our day, but also backwards to the beginning of time. This is because the work of Christ on the Cross in an *eschatological* act, that is, it is a work done at a moment of time that belongs to eternity; and in eternity there is no past, present or future. Christ is the same, yesterday, today, and for ever. A consequence of this reality is that the Church is not just 2000 years old, but is as ancient as man himself. See Gen. 4:26.

As time went on, Israel thought back to the goodness of God in her history and in her experience of life. One of the great commands of God in both the Old and the New Testaments is "Remember!" God had rescued his people from the grip of

Pharaoh, had brought them through the Red Sea and then through the parched wilderness. And while there, at Mount Sinai, he had given them his *Torah,* his teaching, or, as we have seen, the revelation of his mind. Then he had crowned his kindness by giving them a land to call their own. At Sinai he had also bestowed upon them a *Covenant* of love and made total commitment to them. This Covenant was founded upon grace alone, that is to say, it was all done by a loving God to a people that in no way could be said to deserve it.

All that God had asked in return was that they should "obey my voice and keep my covenant" (Exod. 19:5). Since God's "voice" was expressed in any or all of his commandments that reveal his Word, this meant that, if Israel broke God's law in any way at all, then Israel was committing nothing less than *lese majesty,* treason against her sovereign Lord and God. Her sins in his sight were thus no mere peccadillos. They were signs of a basic unfaithfulness, even of treachery on the part of the second party to the Covenant. Verse 15 describes these sins of inadvertence as "a breach of faith". Some of these sins are:

(1) Disloyalty to a neighbour who has got himself into trouble, by refusing to testify on his behalf in a law-court.

(2) Inadvertent misappropriation of sacred property.

(3) Refusal to acknowledge that one has made oneself unclean. (The whole question of uncleanness comes up in full in chapters 11–15.)

(4) Refusal to acknowledge that one has uttered a rash oath.

We note that there is no line drawn here between breaking a ritual law, and so being disloyal to God's Word, and a personal disloyalty to one's neighbour! This is because in Old Testament thinking, unlike that of Plato, Aristotle and the Greeks in general, there is no line between matter and spirit, heaven and earth, body and soul, law and grace, or anything else. All creation is *one* simply on the ground that God himself is *one.*

Naturally God takes Israel's sin seriously, since the doing of sin is a personal attack against God's gracious and loving will for Israel. To a man, an inadvertent sin may appear to be quite unimportant. But God actually "smells" an odour of it in his nostrils, that is to say, it comes right up into the very experience of his own person and *affects* him. Human sin reaches God, it touches him, it hurts him, it moves him. But what happens is that it moves him to be deeply compassionate, and so God is ready to forgive man despite man's insolent attack upon the revelation of his will and loving purpose.

Yet man first has to *want* to be forgiven; second must be willing to make some kind of retribution for his folly; and third, must make confession of his sin. If, however, even so small an item as a pigeon is beyond a simple man's resources to offer up, then a mere cupful of flour even without the addition of olive oil, a commodity that was much less expensive than the frankincense that was brought in from abroad, would suffice for the offering he had to make. How gracious, understanding and merciful this God is whom we meet with here. Just a mere cupful of flour for the sin of your soul! *And he shall be forgiven* (v. 13). What a God this is!

LESE MAJESTY

Leviticus 5:14–6:7

The Lord said to Moses, "If anyone commits a breach of faith and sins unwittingly in any of the holy things of the Lord, he shall bring, as his guilt offering to the Lord, a ram without blemish out of the flock, valued by you in shekels of silver, according to the shekel of the sanctuary; it is a guilt offering. He shall also make restitution for what he has done amiss in the holy thing, and shall add a fifth to it and give it to the priest; and the priest shall make atonement for him with the ram of the guilt offering, and he shall be forgiven.

"If any one sins, doing any of the things which the Lord has commanded not to be done, though he does not know it, yet he is guilty and shall bear his iniquity. He shall bring to the priest a ram without blemish out of the flock, valued by you at the price for a guilt offering, and the priest shall make atonement for him for the error which he committed unwittingly, and he shall be forgiven. It is a guilt offering; he is guilty before the Lord."

The Lord said to Moses, "If any one sins and commits a breach of faith against the Lord by deceiving his neighbour in a matter of deposit or security, or through robbery, or if he has oppressed his neighbour or has found what was lost and lied about it, swearing falsely—in any of all the things which men do and sin therein, when one has sinned and become guilty, he shall restore what he took by robbery, or what he got by oppression, or the deposit which was committed to him, or the lost thing which he found, or anything about which he has sworn falsely; he shall restore it in full, and shall add a fifth to it, and give it to him to whom it belongs, on the day of his guilt offering. And he shall bring to the priest his guilt offering to the Lord, a ram without blemish out of the flock, valued by you at the price for a guilt offering; and the priest shall make atonement for him before the Lord, and he shall be forgiven for any of the things which one may do and thereby become guilty."

But the essence of disloyalty is sin directed against the Person of God himself, for that is a breaking of the very covenant that God himself laid upon Israel at Sinai. The "fine" that God exacted for such a crime could be quite expensive, even if the "sin" was just not paying the offerings and tithes due to God. At Exod. 30:11-16 we are told that the head of each family was expected to pay half a sanctuary shekel per annum, let us say, something like merely a dollar in value. Incidentally, the value of the sacrificial animal for the purpose of fining was also reckoned in shekels (5:15). We read about the application of this fine in 2 Kings 12:16.

The cost of the beast brought as a guilt offering was meant to hurt. We have come across a new word, *asham* (guilt-offering). It is the name of a kind of offering which we must keep in mind as we proceed. The root of the word has to deal with the idea of restitution for any desecration of the holy, and so means something like "reparation". And it carries within it the (God-given) power actually to avert the wrath of God! Another hint of God's marvellous grace and goodness! To feel guilty, then, means to be conscious of your liability to repay. It means knowing that you are in a state of debt. We should compare this with the words of Jesus which he used in giving us the Lord's Prayer: "Forgive us our debts" (Matt. 6:12).

Another word to look at occurs in verse 15. Here a common verb is used in a unique way. "He shall bring" means "he shall restore" (all one word in Hebrew), as we see from Num. 5:7, thus putting the emphasis upon the restitution necessary for a "breach of faith"—another term used only in this special way. The idea of a breach of faith gets right down from outward actions to the very heart of the matter. The horror of the possible extent of such a breach is illustrated when the word occurs again at 20:3. For there a man is said to profane God's holy name by sacrificing one of his babies to the Canaanite god Molech, right beside the walls of the holy city of Jerusalem!

DEALING WITH THE GUILTY PARTY

Leviticus 5:14–6:7 (*cont'd*)

If a man is arrested for cheating in a financial deal with another, or has robbed him, or has taken something of his by force, then he must restore what he has taken along with an added 20% of its value. That is the first step he has to take, the legal action. We read about this in Exod. 22:7–15. But step two is this: on the day that he pays for the damage he has done he must go to the sanctuary with a blemish-free ram and have the priest sacrifice it for him. The legal side of things and the moral and spiritual side are here all one. For as we see at verse 1, to sin against your neighbour is to commit a breach of faith against the Lord! How many people think that way today in their business life?

What we meet with in the Law of Moses is something very different from modern legal practice. The Old Testament makes it clear that God has made man a free creature, free to choose between right and wrong. Thus, normally, no one must deprive his neighbour of his freedom; in fact not even the magistrate has the right to do so. Shutting up a man in prison

for his misdeeds is something unknown in the Old Testament.
Again, how many people today are aware of that? What we do
find is that the thief or the hooligan must repay the man he has
injured by working hard to earn the necessary money, and give
that back to the man he has injured—plus 20%!

His unneighbourly act might be a very serious one indeed.
Not only might he have wronged another man, he might even
deny that he ever did so under oath (i.e. "against the Lord"). In
such a case then the Lord has been deliberately made an
accomplice in the fraud. This is no less than a desecration of the
divine Name. How seriously the Old Testament takes every
word that people utter! We remember what Jesus said: "Do not
swear at all, either by heaven, for it is the throne of God, or by
the earth, for it is his footstool ... Let what you say be simply
'Yes' or 'No'" (Matt. 5:34–37).

But the act of restitution which he must make must be
coupled (because the two things take place at the same time)
with confession of his sin to God. So the offender must first be
led to "feel guilty". The phrase runs, "On the day when he feels
guilt", that is, at the moment in his experience of life when it
really comes home to him that he is a sinner in the sight of God.
Thus the *asham,* which God in his grace has legislated, and
which the sinner then brings, is the means of grace that God has
provided by which a man may repent of his evil and find
forgiveness and renewal.

Let us notice this, however. Such an act by a priest to produce
atonement has also been ordered by God himself so as to be
made use of in just such situations as this. This act really
becomes a sort of absolution. That is because the sacrifice, the
asham, which the priest offers on behalf of the guilty party, (and
remember, by laying his hands on the head of the beast, the
guilty person has identified himself with it), now actually
performs, accomplishes, the will of God. Indeed, it is God
himself who has ordered this to be so (6:1). And so the *asham*
becomes effective, and fulfils the will of God to absolve the
guilty one of his sin. God's pardon has *reached* the chastened
sinner.

The order of events found here therefore is as follows:

(a) confession;
(b) reparation;
(c) forgiveness;
(d) absolution.

THE UNSPEAKABLE MERCY OF GOD

Let us go back to what we said at 4:1. There we noted that there was a class of sin for which the Law provided no means of atonement. Swearing a false oath belonged to this class, for it was a sin, not just against man, but against God himself. It was something like the blasphemy against the Holy Spirit that Jesus speaks of in Matt. 12:31–32. There was only one punishment possible for such insolence, and that was death (Num. 15:30). And yet that terrible statement is not the end of the matter. It is true that the death penalty for "sins with a high hand" is indeed the *righteous* judgment of Israel's *righteous* God, even as the total obliteration of the world of men was God's only possible *righteous* decision in the days of Noah (Gen. 6:5–7). We witness here however the unspeakable *mercy* of God, who is not bound by his own laws and decrees. The procedure we have just looked at actually offers such a sinner the atonement and forgiveness which the Law of Moses prescribed only for sins of inadvertence. So we reach the amazing conclusion that God's righteous judgement is at the same time his boundless mercy and grace (Gen. 6:17–18).

One of the "sins with a high hand" for which no atonement was available was murder. We recognize that the crucifixion of Jesus, legally speaking, was the murder of an innocent man. Yet what do we hear Jesus saying out of the pain and horror of the Cross? His words are these: "Father, forgive them, for they are committing a sin which should be regarded as merely one of inadvertence"! Such then is the *righteous,* judgmental compassion and forgiveness of the God about whom we learn in both the Old and the New Testaments.

INSTRUCTIONS FOR THE PRIESTS (Text)

Leviticus 6:8–7:38

The Lord said to Moses, "Command Aaron and his sons, saying, This is the law of the burnt offering. The burnt offering shall be on the hearth upon the altar all night until the morning, and the fire of the altar shall be kept burning on it. And the priest shall put on his linen garment, and put his linen breeches upon his body, and he shall take up the ashes to which the fire has consumed the burnt offering on the altar, and put them beside the altar. Then he shall put off his garments, and put on other garments, and carry forth the ashes outside the camp to a clean place. The fire on the altar shall be kept burning on it, it shall not go out; the priest shall burn wood on it every morning, and he shall lay the burnt offering in order upon it, and shall burn on it the fat of the peace offerings. Fire shall be kept burning upon the altar continually; it shall not go out.

"And this is the law of the cereal offering. The sons of Aaron shall offer it before the Lord, in front of the altar. And one shall take from it a handful of the fine flour of the cereal offering with its oil and all the frankincense which is on the cereal offering, and burn this as its memorial portion on the altar, a pleasing odour to the Lord. And the rest of it Aaron and his sons shall eat; it shall be eaten unleavened in a holy place; in the court of the tent of meeting they shall eat it. It shall not be baked with leaven. I have given it as their portion of my offerings by fire; it is a thing most holy, like the sin offering and the guilt offering. Every male among the children of Aaron may eat of it, as decreed for ever throughout your generations, from the Lord's offerings by fire; whoever touches them shall become holy."

The Lord said to Moses, "This is the offering which Aaron and his sons shall offer to the Lord on the day when he is anointed: a tenth of an ephah of fine flour as a regular cereal offering, half of it in the morning and half in the evening. It shall be made with oil on a griddle; you shall bring it well mixed, in baked pieces like a cereal offering, and offer it to the Lord as decreed for ever; the whole of it shall be burned. Every cereal offering of a priest shall be wholly burned; it shall not be eaten."

The Lord said to Moses, "Say to Aaron and his sons, This is the law of the sin offering. In the place where the burnt offering is killed shall the sin offering be killed before the Lord; it is most holy. The priest who offers it for sin shall eat it; in a holy place it shall be eaten, in the court of the tent of meeting. Whatever touches its flesh shall be holy; and when any of its blood is sprinkled on a garment, you shall wash that on which it was sprinkled in a holy place. And the earthen vessel in which it is boiled shall be broken; but if it is boiled in a bronze vessel, that shall be scoured, and rinsed in water. Every male among the priests may eat of it; it is most holy. But no sin offering shall be eaten from which any blood is brought into the tent of meeting to make atonement in the holy place; it shall be burned with fire.

"This is the law of the guilt offering. It is most holy; in the place where they kill the burnt offering they shall kill the guilt offering, and its blood shall be thrown on the altar round about. And all its fat shall be offered, the fat tail, the fat that covers the entrails, the two kidneys with the fat that is on them at the loins, and the appendage of the liver which he shall take away with the kidneys; the priest shall burn them on the altar as an offering by fire to the Lord; it is a guilt offering. Every male among the priests may eat of it; it shall be eaten in a holy place; it is most holy. The guilt offering is like the sin offering, there is one law for them; the priest who makes atonement with it shall have it. And the priest who offers any man's burnt offering shall have for himself the skin of the burnt offering which he has offered. And every cereal offering baked in the oven and all that is prepared on a pan or a griddle shall belong to the priest who offers it. And every cereal offering, mixed with oil or dry, shall be for all the sons of Aaron, one as well as another.

"And this is the law of the sacrifice of peace offerings which one may offer to the Lord. If he offers it for a thanksgiving, then he shall offer with the thank offering unleavened cakes mixed with oil, unleavened wafers spread with oil, and cakes of fine flour well mixed with oil. With the sacrifice of his peace offerings for thanksgiving he shall bring his offering with cakes of leavened bread. And of such he shall offer one cake from each offering, as an offering to the Lord; it shall belong to the priest who throws the blood of the peace offerings. And the flesh of the sacrifice of his peace offerings for thanksgiving shall be eaten on the day of his offering; he shall not leave any of it until the morning. But if the sacrifice of his offering is a votive offering or a freewill offering, it shall be eaten on the day that he offers his sacrifice, and on the morrow what remains of the flesh of it shall be eaten, but what remains of the flesh of the sacrifice on the third day shall be burned with fire. If any of the flesh of the sacrifice of his peace offering is eaten on the third day, he who offers it shall not be accepted, neither shall it be credited to him; it shall be an abomination, and he who eats of it shall bear his iniquity.

"Flesh that touches any unclean thing shall not be eaten; it shall be burned with fire. All who are clean may eat flesh, but the person who eats of the flesh of the sacrifice of the Lord's peace offerings while an uncleanness is on him, that person shall be cut off from his people. And if any one touches an unclean thing, whether the uncleanness of man or an unclean beast or any unclean abomination, and then eats of the flesh of the sacrifice of the Lord's peace offerings, that person shall be cut off from his people."

The Lord said to Moses, "Say to the people of Israel, You shall eat no fat, of ox, or sheep, or goat. The fat of an animal that dies of itself, and the fat of one that is torn by beasts, may be put to any other use, but on no account shall you eat it. For every person who eats of the fat of an animal of which an offering by fire is made to the Lord shall be cut off from his people."

The Lord said to Moses, "Say to the people of Israel, He that offers the sacrifice of his peace offerings to the Lord shall bring his offering to the Lord; from the sacrifice of his peace offerings he shall bring with his own hands the offerings by fire to the Lord; he shall bring the fat with the breast, that the breast may be waved as a wave offering before the Lord. The priest shall burn the fat on the altar, but the breast shall be for Aaron and his sons. And the right thigh you shall give to the priest as an offering from the sacrifice of your peace offering; he among the sons of Aaron who offers blood of the peace offerings and the fat shall have the right thigh of a portion. For the breast that is waved and the thigh that is offered I have taken from the people of Israel, out of the sacrifices of their peace offerings, and have given them to Aaron the priest and to his sons, as a perpetual due from the people of Israel. This is the portion of Aaron and of his sons from the offerings made by fire to the Lord, consecrated to them on the day they were presented to serve as priests of the Lord; the Lord commanded this to be given them by the people of Israel, on the day that they were anointed; it is a perpetual due throughout their generations."

This is the law of the burnt offering, of the cereal offering, of the sin offering, of the guilt offering, of the consecration, and of the peace offerings, which the Lord commanded Moses on Mount Sinai, on the day that he commanded the people of Israel to bring their offerings to the Lord, in the wilderness of Sinai.

INSTRUCTIONS FOR THE PRIESTS (Commentary) I

Leviticus 6:8-7:38 (*cont'd*)

This section goes over the various kinds of offering and sacrifice we have met and gives instructions to the priests about their administration.

THE HOLOCAUST (6:8-13) (see chapter 1)

The word for this kind of sacrifice is *'olah*. This Hebrew word describes a sacrifice that goes up whole to God, and so is what may be called a "holocaust", meaning literally "whole-burning". This sacrifice was something extra special. So the priest had to be extra specially careful about what he wore when he officiated at it (see Exod. 28:40-42). As we read through the Old Testament we discover how this special ritual gradually grew up round the holocaust to emphasize its special nature. The special garment of the priest was meant to impress upon the worshipper the awesomeness of God's presence, though that could only be rendered symbolically. The priest actually changed his vestments twice over during the course of the offering he was presenting to God.

First of all, the fire on the altar was never allowed to go out, since it was meant to remind us that we are wholly and continually sinful; we are sinful not just at intervals, so to speak, but all the time; and therefore we need to be kept right with God morning and evening, day and night (see Exod. 29:38-42; Num. 28:3-8).

Secondly, in earlier centuries God had shown Moses that his holy presence was to be found in fire. He did so symbolically when Moses witnessed a bush that burned but was not consumed (Exod. 3:1-6). Moses had thus discovered that God was present with his chosen son, Israel (Exod. 4:22), right in the fires of suffering in Egypt. How strange a thing to relate about God: that God himself was in the fires! But of course, being the living God, he was not consumed. So it came about that both priests and prophets declared to Israel that if only they would cling to

God they too would not be consumed—though God himself was the fire. What a paradox in our way of thinking about God! But it was not we human beings who thought up this paradox, it was God himself. This is the constant teaching of the Old Testament, as we see from such passages as Isa. 43:1-3 and Dan. 3:19-28.

Thirdly, there is another way of thinking about all this. We have said that, since God is himself the living God, we cannot say that he could be consumed. Yet God himself *is* a consuming fire, to use the phrase we find the great prophets using, as at Isa. 10:17; 30-27; 31:9; 33:14: Deut. 4:24. The theology of this strange reality is expounded here in Leviticus with total clarity. When the ordinary man stood watching an *'olah* go up in flames, this total and never-ceasing sacrifice represented what was in the heart of the living God himself.

Finally, we should set the *meaning* of the holocaust offering alongside the *meaning* of the peace offering, which we looked at in an earlier chapter. For the word peace, *shalom,* also means wholeness and completion. God's *total* judgment, therefore, is not the end of his approach to us poor human beings; for out of his judgment there emerges his *total* renewal, seen in his offer of unity and fellowship (a) between man and the animals (Isa. 11:6-9), (b) between man and man (Mic. 4:4), and (c) between man and God (Isa. 2:1-4).

THE CEREAL OFFERING (6:14-23) (see chapter 2)

The description of the cereal offering reminds us somewhat of our Holy Communion ritual today, for all males present could taste the bread that was being offered. And it had been rendered holy so that, in eating it, the taster was made holy too. Not only so, but God too enjoyed the meal. It reached him sensually, we read here, because its nice smell was something he liked. As we have said before, the Old Testament is not afraid to describe the deepest theological ideas in simple every-day language—the same language that Jesus used when he taught in parables.

The ordination of a priest requires no more valuable an

offering than that required from a layman; in fact, no mention is made at all of the expensive frankincense that we found at verse 15. Does this fact contribute towards the belief held firmly by Israel that when God granted his Covenant to his people, he required that all of them *together* should be his priests, not to each other, but to the pagan world (Exod. 19:6)? Once again, at verse 22 this time, we meet with the idea of "wholeness", through the introduction of a new word, *kalil.* The offering by the priest is to be *kalil,* total. So again it is stressed: (a) God's judgment is upon the entire people of Israel; (b) it is a total judgment; (c) therefore, because God is God and not man, his mercy can only be total also.

THE SIN OFFERING (6:24–30) (see chs. 4:1–5:13)

The idea of holiness undoubtedly arose in very ancient times and represented a kind of taboo. A god could punish a man for example, if he happened merely to tread on "holy" ground by mistake. But here it is the holiness of the God of redeeming love that is contagious. What a wonderful idea this is. We are thrilled to discover how the experience of it grows in depths of meaning throughout the biblical story. God's holy love spills over into our lives! The last verse of the chapter emphasizes what we noted earlier, that blood is sacred, because the blood, to the sacramental way of thinking, is life itself. Accordingly, the sacredness of all life which God has created is underlined most strongly.

INSTRUCTIONS FOR THE PRIESTS (Commentary) II

Leviticus 6:8–7:38 *(cont'd)*

THE GUILT OFFERING (7:1–10) (see chs. 5:14–6:7)

It is deeply moving for us to discover that, in the case where a man seeks for atonement for his sin once he has confessed his guilt, his offering is looked upon as the holiest of all offerings. The Law of Moses is not a mere dry-as-dust legal code. It concerns itself with a man's personal relationship with God and rejoices when a man repents and desires to return to fellowship with the Lord. Moreover, it remembers that the labourer is worthy of his hire. The priest is to share in the "whole" goodness of God, when he offers the '*olah*. For he is allowed to keep the animal's skin.

THE PEACE OFFERINGS (7:11–27) (see ch. 3)

The rituals described here, and at 22:21-23; 29-30, distinguish three kinds of communion sacrifice. These are:

(1) The sacrifice of praise, *todah,* offered on certain solemn occasions.

(2) The freewill sacrifice, *nedabah,* offered out of sheer exuberance of heart and in gratitude to God for all his goodness and love.

(3) The votive sacrifice, *neder,* which the offerer had already promised to make, and he must now fulfil. All three were joyous acts of communion with God. Since they were meant to maintain or renew fellowship with the "holy" God, might we dare call them forms of "holy communion"?

The peace offering should include in its "menu" all kinds of delicacies, all of which would be made by the fair hands of a man's wife and daughters, so that they too could share in his joy—and God's. And the priest is to share in this also, for he is to take home to his wife and children some of the goodies that the other families have made for the occasion. This sense of joy is expressed also when votive and free-will offerings are made. There are however, certain divinely uttered directives connected with these sacrifices. People must not eat meat which has gone putrid, or which has become ceremonially unclean, or eat of the sacrificial beast so long as they themselves are unprepared in heart and mind. These divine commands are very understandable.

There is one theological comment that we can make here, however. Decomposition of the carcass was believed to have set in by the third day (v.17). Any flesh eaten that day will not be acceptable to God, nor will the offerer be acceptable, either to God or to his fellow-men (v.20). His sacrifice will simply not be effective, but will be regarded as an abomination, and he will continue to "bear his iniquity". At Hosea 6:2 the prophet points out that Israel as a people has been the victim of God's righteous judgment, and so Hosea calls upon his people to return to the Lord before decomposition sets in. So the words of Leviticus here form an acted parable to help Hosea in his preaching! But more than that–they lead us to see the real power of God. For he raised Jesus from the dead on the first day after the body's decomposition had set in. This is just what the Psalmist prayed God would not need to do (Ps. 16:10, Authorised Version).

Animal fat was never to be eaten. We remember reading at 3:16 the words, "All fat is the Lord's". So if a man found himself eating a roast at home with his family, that is to say, just having an ordinary meal together, one that was not a special ceremonial in which God shared, even then, or especially then, he must not eat the fat; for he could not give it to God as he could at the altar. The same was true if he should taste the meat of an animal he had come across just newly dead.

THE WAVE OFFERING (7:28–38)

Now we meet with still another technical term, the "wave offering". Why the priest was to wave an animal's breast "before the Lord" is not clear, or why even the breast alone. The action here may belong in the ceremony of the peace offering that we met in chapter 3. If the breast was waved towards the altar and back again, then it may have symbolized for the ordinary worshipper the idea that when God asks him for his offering, he is to give it willingly. But once it has been given, God will be glad to hand it back to him for his own use, and to feed the family. Note that in verse 34, for the first time in Leviticus, God actually speaks in the first person: "The breast and the thigh I have taken from the people of Israel . . . and given them . . . to the priests". These are to be their rightful wages for all time. So we have a kind of wave offering from people to priest, and back again. And the first personal speech of God helps to make it very emphatic.

Verses 37–38 are a concluding index to what has preceded.

SETTING UP ISRAEL'S WORSHIP (Text)

Leviticus 8:1–36

The Lord said to Moses, "Take Aaron and his sons with him, and the garments, and the anointing oil, and the two rams, and the basket of unleavened bread; and assemble all the congregation at the door of the tent of meeting."

And Moses did as the Lord commanded him; and the congregation was assembled at the door of the tent of meeting. And Moses said to the congregation, "This is the thing which the Lord has commanded to be done." And Moses brought Aaron and his sons, and washed them with water. And he put on him the coat, and girded him with the girdle, and clothed him with the robe, and put the ephod upon him, and girded him with the skilfully woven band of the ephod, binding it to him therewith. And he placed the breast-piece on him, and in the breast-piece he put the Urim and the Thummin. And he set the turban upon his head, and on the turban, in front, he set the golden plate, the holy crown, as the Lord commanded Moses.

Then Moses took the anointing oil, and anointed the tabernacle and all that was in it, and consecrated them. And he sprinkled some of it on the altar seven times, and anointed the altar and all its utensils, and the laver on its base, to consecrate them. And he poured some of the anointing oil on Aaron's head, and anointed him, to consecrate him. And Moses brought Aaron's sons, and clothed them with coats, and girded them with girdles, and bound caps on them, as the Lord commanded Moses.

Then he brought the bull of the sin offering; and Aaron and his sons laid their hands upon the head of the bull of the sin offering. And Moses killed it, and took the blood, and with his finger put it on the horns of the altar round about, and purified the altar, and poured out the blood at the base of the altar, and consecrated it, to make atonement for it. And he took all the fat that was on the entrails, and the appendage of the liver, and the two kidneys with their fat, and Moses burned them on the altar. But the bull, and its skin, and its flesh, and its dung, he burned with fire outside the camp, as the Lord commanded Moses.

Then he presented the ram of the burnt offering; and Aaron and his sons laid their hands on the head of the ram. And Moses killed it, and threw the blood upon the altar round about. And when the ram was cut into pieces, Moses burned the head and the pieces and the fat. And when the entrails and the legs were washed with water, Moses burned the whole ram on the altar, as a burnt offering, a pleasing odour, an offering by fire to the Lord, as the Lord commanded Moses.

Then he presented the other ram, the ram of ordination; and Aaron and his sons laid their hands on the head of the ram. And Moses killed it, and took some of its blood and put it on the tip of Aaron's right ear and on the thumb of his right hand and on the great toe of his right foot. And Aaron's sons were brought, and Moses put some of the blood on the tips of their right ears and on the thumbs of their right hands and on the great toes of their right feet; and Moses threw the blood upon the altar round about. Then he took the fat, and the fat tail, and all the fat that was on the entrails, and the appendage of the liver, and the two kidneys with their fat, and the right thigh; and out of the basket of unleavened bread which was before the Lord he took one unleavened cake, and one cake of bread with oil, and one wafer, and placed them on the fat and on the right thigh; and he put all these in the hands of his sons, and waved them as a wave offering before the Lord. Then Moses took them from their hands, and burned them on the altar with the burnt offering, as an ordination offering, a pleasing odour, an offering by fire to the Lord. And Moses took the breast, and waved it for a wave offering before the Lord; it was Moses' portion of the ram of ordination, as the Lord commanded Moses.

Then Moses took some of the anointing oil and of the blood which was on the altar, and sprinkled it upon Aaron and his garments, and also upon his sons and his sons' garments; so he consecrated Aaron and his garments, and his sons and his sons' garments with him.

And Moses said to Aaron and his sons, "Boil the flesh at the door of the tent of meeting, and there eat it and the bread that is in the basket of ordination offerings, as I commanded, saying, 'Aaron and his sons shall eat it'; and what remains of the flesh and the bread you shall burn with fire. And you shall not go out from the door of the tent of meeting for seven days, until the days of your ordination are completed, for it will take seven days to ordain you. As has been done today, the Lord has commanded to be done to make atonement for you. At the door of the tent of meeting you shall remain day and night for seven days, performing what the Lord has charged, lest you die; for so I am commanded." And Aaron and his sons did all the things which the Lord commanded by Moses.

SETTING UP ISRAEL'S WORSHIP (Commentary)

Leviticus 8:1-36 *(cont'd)*

Chapters 8-10 describe the inauguration of Israel's worship in the Wilderness. The priest held a special position amongst the People of the Covenant. In the first place, in his wisdom, God had chosen to speak to Israel at a special place, or in special places, not just anywhere, as we have seen. Then secondly, God had chosen to do this through particular people who were specially set apart for this purpose. These were the priests. They were regarded as the descendants of Aaron, the brother of Moses. So when we read the word "Aaron", from now on we are to understand by it all priests from his day onwards. Perhaps we can understand this better when we remember that all the people of Israel are actually called by the name of their ancestor, Jacob (Gen. 32:28; Ps. 44:4; Isa. 2:5).

In the book of Exodus we read how God called Moses to be the medium of his "Word", and how God promised to be with him in all that he had to *say* (Exod. 3:12; 4:12). What he had to *say* might at this point be summed up in the Ten Commandments (Exod. 20:1-17—and note v.1). But God also *said* to Moses many things in connection with Israel's worship, about building the sanctuary, how it was to be furnished, and so on. Moreover, as part of what he said about these matters, he promised to be present with Israel, his people, at that special *place* where the worship was to be carried on for generations to come. It was "Aaron" who was given the responsibility for this whole area of God's chosen means of maintaining fellowship with his people (see Exod. 28–29).

It was in order to make clear to the people the importance of the task of the priests that they wore the vestments mentioned in verses 7–9. Some of these garments may have been part of the royal regalia before the line of David was wiped out in 587 B.C; for till that date it was the king who was the real head of the cult. It was only after 515 B.C., when the Temple had been rebuilt and consecrated, that the familiar figure of the High Priest, with whom we meet in the New Testament also, takes over.

He was magnificently apparelled. He wore:

(a) A *coat,* that is, some kind of under garment

(b) A *belt* to hold it in. So the coat must have been something like a cassock today

(c) Over the "cassock" he wore a *robe.* It would correspond to the gown worn today. It was bright blue in colour.

(d) Over the "gown" the High Priest wore an *ephod.* It was tied on with a "skilfully woven band". We have to use our imagination to picture what it was like, for we do not know for sure. This ephod, however, was probably something like an apron. In one of its pockets, which were placed "over the heart", the High Priest carried the dacred *dice.*

(e) These dice were known as *Urim* and *Thummim.* No one knows exactly what these two words mean. We can make a good guess, however, at connecting them with two Hebrew words that mean *Yes* and *No.* Evidently the priest could throw the dice "before the Lord" in order to discover God's will when enquiring what course of action should be taken on special occasions.

(f) He also wore a *turban.* On the front of it was a *plate of pure gold,* with the words *Holy to the Lord* engraved on it. In this way God was teaching Israel to develop the meaning of the word "holy". As can be seen at Zech. 14:20–21, a late passage belonging to the time of the Second Temple, the prophet was looking to the day when the utensils in the homes of the "holy families" that comprised Israel would be just as holy as the plates used by the priests described here in Leviticus.

What we read about being holy in this passage is told in more detail in the book of Exodus. But it is repeated here at this point to make clear to Israel that she is not only to *become* God's "holy nation" (Exod. 19:5), she is also to *remain* his holy nation for ever, *wholly*. To make this clear we read of a symbolic act. It was sufficient to anoint Aaron's *beard* alone (v. 12); for the head of a man represents the whole of the body. Paul makes use of this way of thinking when he describes the relationship of Christ to his Church. This action is followed by the offering of an *'olah,* a *whole* offering (v. 18).

Being a sinner just like other men, the priest had first to offer a special sin offering for himself before he could be ordained (see 4:1–12). We note the mystical use of "seven times" once again. It will take a whole week, seven days, just as God took seven days to create the world, to complete the "creation" of the High Priest, his consecration. And during that period the poor ordinands had to be fed; so provision had to be made for that very mundane activity also! Only after this long period could the priest put on his fine vestments. Even the altar and the other furnishings, we read, needed an act of atonement before they could be used. This was because all man's possessions and implements, even the soil he treads (Gen. 4:11), are infected by his sinful rebellious state of heart and mind. For man tends to believe that he can live the full life without respect to the revelation of the living God.

Priests are not like the proverbial curate's egg, good in parts and bad in parts. They belong to the human race. They are wholly sinful, as are all men, from the tip of their ears to their thumbs and big toes (v.23). Consecration to the priesthood is therefore an act of grace on God's part. No person selected to be consecrated a priest ever deserves the position. All he can do is obey God's instructions in every detail. For everything man touches and handles is rendered unholy by doing so. Even the offerings of foodstuffs that were brought for the occasion had to be consecrated before they could be used at the ceremony (v. 26–29), and the vestments that the priest wore had to be "fumigated" from the contagion of sinful hands (v.30).

Finally, in verse 27 we read that Moses placed "the whole" into Aaron's hands, making the priesthood responsible for this entire area of God's revealed "Word" spoken to Israel. The idea is expressed in Hebrew by "the ram that filled his hands", a symbolical way of showing that the priest had received this authority. Today we "fill the hands" of an ordinand by placing in them a Bible.

This sacrifice of the ram of ordination formed the climax to the whole series of ceremonies. It was in reality what we today would call a communion meal. God above tastes the sacrificial meal that has come up to him as "a pleasing odour" (v.28). Man below eats the consecrated food, and so actually does on earth what God does in heaven. That is fellowship indeed, and every aspect of it comes from grace alone.

THE MEANING OF "TODAY"

Leviticus 8:1–36 (*cont'd*)

Verse 34 reads: "As has been done today, the Lord has commanded to be done to make atonement". This use of *today* is no casual term, and does not mean merely "this 24 hours". Its use is what scholars call "the cultic present". At the moment of fellowship between God and man, when man receives total forgiveness and total reconciliation with God, the eternal *meaning* of the sacrificial act is made plain. The act becomes significant *now* because it belongs to eternity. It is significant not for the future, for a heaven that lies beyond death, but for *now,* for the now of the God who is eternal himself, the same yesterday, today and for ever.

The technical term we apply to this revealed idea is "eschatological". Eschatology in the Old Testament does not refer, as in other religions, to what will happen at the end of time, or even after this world is rolled up like a roller blind. The term means that, as Paul puts it, *now* is the day of salvation, not at some future period beyond death as the spiritualist might conjecture. This is because this *now*, this *today,* on earth, is like the eye of a telescope through which one can see the eternal purposes of God which are outside time and space—and see them now! Once again we discover how Leviticus provided the New Testament writers with what they wanted and needed when they theologized on the significance of the Cross of Christ. For they would remember that Jesus himself used this word "today" in the way that Leviticus uses it (Luke 13:32–33; 19:42).

However, there is still another important issue that arises for the Christian faith from this and other chapters in Leviticus. It concerns the Old Testament view of human personality as one whole (*nephesh* is the Hebrew word). Man is not a soul dwelling temporarily in a body, a belief basic both to Greek thought and to the Eastern religions, and which has infected the theology of some of the sects that abound today. Without this theological view of the unity of the human personality which is unique to the Bible, the New Testament could never have rejoiced in the fact of the resurrection of Christ. It could only have declared what the many religions of the Near East were saying anyway in the first century about the fate of the dead, that immortality of the soul is all that we can read into the last chapters of the Gospels.

MAKING ATONEMENT (Text)

Leviticus 9:1–24

On the eighth day Moses called Aaron and his sons and the elders of Israel; and he said to Aaron, "Take a bull calf for a sin offering, and a ram for a burnt offering, both without blemish, and offer them before the Lord. And say to the people of Israel, 'Take a male goat for a sin offering, and a calf and a lamb, both a year old without blemish, for a burnt offering, and an ox and a ram for peace offerings, to sacrifice before the Lord, and a cereal offering mixed with oil; for today the Lord will appear to you.'" And they brought what Moses commanded before the tent of meeting; and all the congregation drew near and stood before the Lord. And Moses said, "This is the thing which the Lord commanded you to do; and the glory of the Lord will appear to you." Then Moses said to Aaron, "Draw near to the altar, and offer your sin offering and your burnt offering, and make atonement for yourself and for the people; and bring the offering of the people, and make atonement for them; as the Lord has commanded."

So Aaron drew near to the altar, and killed the calf of the sin offering, which was for himself. And the sons of Aaron presented the blood to him, and he dipped his finger in the blood and put it on the horns of the altar, and poured out the blood at the base of the altar; but the fat and the kidneys and the appendage of the liver from the sin offering he burned upon the altar, as the Lord commanded Moses. The flesh and the skin he burned with fire outside the camp.

And he killed the burnt offering; and Aaron's sons delivered to him the blood, and he threw it on the altar round about. And they delivered the burnt offering to him, piece by piece, and the head; and he burned them upon the altar. And he washed the entrails and the legs, and burned them with the burnt offering on the altar.

Then he presented the people's offering, and took the goat of the sin offering which was for the people, and killed it, and offered it for sin, like the first sin offering. And he presented the burnt offering, and offered it according to the ordinance. And he presented the cereal offering, and filled his hand from it, and burned it upon the altar, besides the burnt offering of the morning.

He killed the ox also and the ram, the sacrifice of peace offerings for the people, and Aaron's sons delivered to him the blood, which he threw upon the altar round about, and the fat of the ox and the ram, the fat tail and that which covers the entrails, and the kidneys, and the appendage of the liver; and they put the fat upon the altar, but the breasts and the right thigh Aaron waved for a wave offering before the Lord; as Moses commanded.

Then Aaron lifted up his hands toward the people and blessed them; and he came down from offering the sin offering and the burnt offering and the peace offerings. And Moses and Aaron went into the tent of meeting; and when they came out they blessed the people, and the glory of the Lord appeared to all the people. And fire came forth from before the Lord and consumed the burnt offering and the fat upon the altar; and when all the people saw it, they shouted, and fell on their faces.

MAKING ATONEMENT (Commentary)

Leviticus 9:1–24 (*cont'd*)

When the whole week needed for the consecration of the priests was over, then came the turn of the rest of the people of Israel. We are to remember that in Leviticus we do not have a photographic description, so to speak, of what took place in the days of the Wilderness wanderings. Our priestly authors believed that God had revealed to Moses the *type* of consecration that Israel was to know as a whole nation later on and down the centuries. The fulness of God's "instructions" therefore are embodied here in this ideal picture of what happened during the period when Moses and Aaron were leading to the Promised Land that rabble of emancipated slaves, that "mixed multitude", which came out of Egypt—Hebrews, Edomites, Sudanese, Egyptians, Kenites and more (Exod. 12:38). These very different cultural groups had all to be welded into one obedient, believing and compassionate people, to be "all one in the Word" that God had spoken, a people that would rejoice to accept God's Covenant of love. For only then would "the glory of the Lord" appear to them (v.6).

This "people of God" was not an ethnic group known as "Jews" at this time. (That name was invented only centuries later, and given to the descendants of the folk in the wilderness by foreigners, Babylonians and Persians.) This is because they are now "holy to the Lord", separated from all ethnic groups, yet containing any ethnic type that would like to join them (see Isa. 56:6), and in consequence they can now be known only by their relationship to God.

The preparation for such a consecration was of great psychological importance. The people had to be "worked up" to a sense of expectancy before they could hope to begin the ceremony. Verses 8-14 insist that the priest must be equally psychologically prepared to perform his special function. Only thereafter (verses 15–21) can come the people's sin offering, the ritual which has been described already in chapters 1–7.

A bull for Aaron's sin represents the expensive offering for the very *responsible* position of the priest, but a goat suffices for the ordinary man. Then follows, as we have seen, the sacrifice of an ox as the people's acceptance of the peace of God. This complicated series of offerings would be conducted in full swing by Ezra's day, and was certainly being enacted when Jesus went up to Jerusalem and entered the Temple.

The long and complicated ceremony ends with what we would call the pronouncing of the benediction, or blessing, of the people. Aaron came down the steps from the high altar and lifted up his hands. Yet it is not Aaron who blesses the people. It is God himself who does so, through Aaron. The latter's uplifted hands are, as it were, laid upon the heads of all the people at once; so in this way his arms come to act as a kind of lightning conductor bearing God's grace from heaven to earth. The words of the benediction are probably what we know as the Aaronic Blessing, to be found at Num. 6:22–26.

Then the lightning did indeed strike, we read. For it burned up the sacrificial animal that was lying upon the altar, and it consumed the "whole" offering which then went up to God. And so the people did indeed see the "glory of God".

Here then, in picture or parabolic language, we have it expressed:

(1) that God does accept the whole-hearted sacrifices of his people;

(2) that sacrifice is God's chosen way of maintaining fellowship with his people;

(3) that the glory of God is made apparent to the mind of man, not just, as the Psalmist says, when "The heavens are telling the glory of God" (Ps. 19:1), but particularly at that *place* and *time* where sacrifice takes place. For it is primarily through sacrifice that the glory of God is revealed. No wonder the New Testament writers came to understand that the glory of God was most fully revealed at that *time* and *place* when Jesus submitted himself willingly to be the sacrifice, ultimate and

whole, which God must exact for the sin of all mankind (John 13:31).

UNHOLY FIRE

Leviticus 10:1–7

Now Nadab and Abihu, the sons of Aaron, each took his censer, and put fire in it, and laid incense on it, and offered unholy fire before the Lord, such as he had not commanded them. And fire came forth from the presence of the Lord and devoured them, and they died before the Lord. Then Moses said to Aaron, "This is what the Lord has said, 'I will show myself holy among those who are near me, and before all the people I will be glorified.'" And Aaron held his peace.

And Moses called Mishael and Elzaphan, the sons of Uzziel the uncle of Aaron, and said to them, "Draw near, carry your brethren from before the sanctuary out of the camp." So they drew near, and carried them in their coats out of the camp, as Moses had said. And Moses said to Aaron and to Eleazar and Ithamar, his sons, "Do not let the hair of your heads hang loose, and do not rend your clothes, lest you die, and lest wrath come upon all the congregation; but your brethren, the whole house of Israel, may bewail the burning which the Lord has kindled. And do not go out from the door of the tent of meeting, lest you die; for the anointing oil of the Lord is upon you." And they did according to the word of Moses.

This little story was not written in the way a twentieth-century author would write. It was written by a Semite, the race of people to whom the Hebrews (and Jesus) belonged. Their culture showed a genius for speaking about what is real and true by means of picture language: myth, poetry, allegory or parable. Many so-called Third World peoples are able to do this, while literally-minded Westerners miss the point of what the Old Testament is saying. This passage belongs with all the other divine instructions which were given to Israel with the express purpose of keeping Israel a people "holy to the Lord". We have seen that the priests had to be consecrated (i.e. "made holy") before they could function in the presence of the holy God; in the same way, too, all the furnishings connected with the worship of Israel had to be rendered holy. And, of course, so did the people. But now the two young men mentioned here think that they know better than God about such things. We learned in chapter 8 that the holy fire was kept going continually on the altar and that it and it alone was to be used for the sacrificial processes that maintained Israel's fellowship with God. For it had come down from God and had not been kindled by the hand of man (9:24). This "holy fire" alone was to be used, "taken from off the altar". Then again, no unsanctified person had the right merely to march into the sanctuary without going through the necessary ritual process before handling the holy things that marked the presence of the holy God.

What these two men—sons of Aaron!—did was this. On a pan filled with hot ashes from an unconsecrated fire taken from somewhere else outside the "holy" precincts, they laid incense which was to go up into God's nostrils as an acted prayer. (The composition of this expensive incense, by the way, is described at Exod. 30:34–38.) This action of theirs was, of course, no mere peccadillo. It was a flagrant piece of disobedience and disloyalty to God. These men were virtually saying, "Our fire is as good as yours, God. We don't need yours." This is an acted parable of the way that secular man thinks about his relationship to God at all times. Their action came under the category of "sins with a high hand", and so was worthy of death. Clearly sons do not necessarily inherit their father's loyalty and eager commitment.

The counterpart of such an action today would be if a man baptized into the Covenant People of God, and thus aware that his relationship to God was one of grace alone, should abandon his baptism and declare that by the use of black magic instead he could draw near to the all-holy God and even compel God by this means to do *his* will—and then actually to teach this to others. "It would be better for him to have a great millstone fastened round his neck and to be drowned in the depth of the sea" (Matt. 18:6), would be an appropriate comment about anyone doing that kind of thing.

And so it did happen. God answered the false fire with the real fire, the fire of his wrath (cf. 9:24). The God of both Testaments is indeed a God who is not mocked (Gal. 6:7). He is not like the modern conception of God so widely held which regards him as a rather kindly old gentleman sitting enthroned "upstairs", who will certainly make everything all right in the end. "Of course he will—for he is love, isn't he?" Both Testaments on the other hand openly speak of God using the image of fire. The figure then represents the awe-ful judgmental nature of the living God. "For the Lord your God is a devouring fire" (Deut. 4:24). But we are to note that the picture of fire is straight away explained by the adjective "jealous". God is passionately, jealously in love with the People of his Covenant, and will permit no one from within Israel or from outside her to disrupt the fellowship he seeks to share with her. Elsewhere we find this extraordinary relationship pictured as that of lover and bride. The God who loves like that naturally refuses to be cuckolded.

Mishael and Elzaphan were cousins of Moses (Exod. 6:22). It is always a pious duty to bury the dead, whether they be good-living people or not. So there they were, wrapped in their priestly vestments, being taken right away from the "holy" sanctuary, as well as away from the encampment of the "holy" people. They were buried "outside the camp", and they were not to be mourned, for no one was to take it that they were on a par with ordinary sinners who yet remained within the Covenant. They too must eventually die, of course, and then be buried decently. What we should really take from this story is a sense of horror at men disobeying the Word of the Lord who is not to be mocked.

THE PRIESTLY REACTION

Leviticus 10:8-20

And the Lord spoke to Aaron, saying, "Drink no wine nor strong drink, you nor your sons with you, when you go into the tent of meeting, lest you die; it shall be a statute for ever throughout your generations. You are to distinguish between the holy and the common, and between the unclean and the clean; and you are to teach the people of Israel all the statutes which the Lord has spoken to them by Moses."

And Moses said to Aaron and to Eleazar and Ithamar, his sons who were left, "Take the cereal offering that remains of the offerings by fire to the Lord, and eat it unleavened beside the altar, for it is most holy; you shall eat it in a holy place, because it is your due and your sons' due, from the offerings by fire to the Lord; for so I am commanded. But the breast that is waved and the thigh that is offered you shall eat in any clean place, you and your sons and your daughters with you; for they are given as your due and your sons' due, from the sacrifices of the peace offerings of the people of Israel. The thigh that is offered and the breast that is waved they shall bring with the offerings by fire of the fat, you wave for a wave offering before the Lord, and it shall be yours, and your sons' with you, as a due for ever; as the Lord has commanded."

Now Moses diligently inquired about the goat of the sin offering, and behold, it was burned! And he was angry with Eleazar and Ithamar, the sons of Aaron who were left, saying, "Why have you not eaten the sin offering in the place of the sanctuary, since it is a thing most holy and has been given to you that you may bear the iniquity of the congregation, to make atonement for them before the Lord? Behold, its blood was not brought into the inner part of the sanctuary. You certainly ought to have eaten it in the sanctuary, as I commanded." And Aaron said to Moses, "Behold, today they have offered their sin offering and their burnt offering before the Lord; and yet such things as these have befallen me! If I had eaten the sin offering today, would it have been acceptable in the sight of the Lord?" And when Moses heard that, he was content.

Conducting a sacrifice when drunk is a form of blasphemy. It is an "unholy" act like those described in chapters 11–15. "Ignorance of the law is no excuse", we say today. Nowhere in the Old Testament is it forbidden to drink alcohol. In fact, wine is God's kindly gift to rejoice the heart of man. Wine can even be seen as a symbol of grace, as Jesus revealed at the wedding in Cana of Galilee. A point that we should remember today however is that in biblical times wine was drunk watered down, some four parts water to one of wine, as is the custom in parts of eastern Europe today. On the other hand, drunkenness is absolutely forbidden to a member of the covenant people of God. Drunkenness is an acted insult at the holy character of human life. The drunken man or woman has reached the point where he or she can no longer make judgments dependent on faith or love.

So the priest was to teach the ordinary people all the statutes (a special word which we shall discuss later) which Moses had learned from God. In practice, in later years, the synagogue was not so much a place of worship like a modern church, as a place of study and learning like a school.

Aaron, Eleazar and Ithamar had of course gone through a frightening experience; accordingly they delicately rejected portions of the sacrificial beast that they could have claimed as their personal wages. Such delicacy of judgment and sensitivity of spirit is not often recorded in a code of law! No wonder we read that when Moses heard their explanation, "he was content".

The stamp of divine approval upon their display of finer feelings is also shown by the double use of the word "today" at verse 19. We have seen that this cultic use of "today" expresses the "eschatological significance" of the act in question. This technical theological term can be clearly understood when we listen to Jesus telling his parable of the "last" judgment (Matt. 25:31–46). There he points out that feeding the hungry *now*, "today", is the last time we can ever feed that particular hungry person, and so also the last time we can turn our eyes away from him. That is why our decision at that "today" is eternal.

CLEAN AND UNCLEAN ANIMALS (Text)

Leviticus 11:1–47

And the Lord said to Moses and Aaron, "Say to the people of Israel, These are the living things which you may eat among all the beasts that are on the earth. Whatever parts the hoof and is cloven-footed and chews the cud, among the animals, you may eat. Nevertheless among those that chew the cud or part the hoof, you shall not eat these: the camel, because it chews the cud but does not part the hoof, is unclean to you. And the rock badger, because it chews the cud but does not part the hoof, is unclean to you. And the hare, because it chews the cud but does not part the hoof, is unclean to you. And the swine, because it parts the hoof and is cloven-footed but does not chew the cud, is unclean to you. Of their flesh you shall not eat, and their carcasses you shall not touch; they are unclean to you.

"These you may eat, of all that are in the waters. Everything in the waters that has fins and scales, whether in the seas or in the rivers, you may eat. But anything in the seas or the rivers that has not fins and scales, of the swarming creatures in the waters and of the living creatures that are in the waters, is an abomination to you. They shall remain an abomination to you; of their flesh you shall not eat, and their carcasses you shall have in abomination. Everything in the waters that has not fins and scales is an abomination to you.

"And these you shall have in abomination among the birds, they shall not be eaten, they are an abomination: the eagle, the vulture, the osprey, the kite, the falcon according to its kind, every raven according to its kind, the ostrich, the nighthawk, the sea gull, the hawk according to its kind, the owl, the cormorant, the ibis, the water hen, the pelican, the carrion vulture, the stork, the heron according to its kind, the hoopoe, and the bat.

"All winged insects that go upon all fours are an abomination to you. Yet among the winged insects that go on all fours you may eat those which have legs above their feet, with which to leap on the earth. Of them you may eat: the locust according to its kind, the bald locust according to its kind, the cricket according to its kind, and the grasshopper according to its kind. But all other winged insects which have four feet are an abomination to you.

"And by these you shall become unclean; whoever touches their carcass shall be unclean until the evening, and whoever carries any part of their carcass shall wash his clothes and be unclean until the evening. Every animal which parts the hoof but is not cloven-footed or does not chew the cud is unclean to you; every one who touches them shall be unclean. And all that go on their paws, among the animals that go on all fours, are unclean to you; whoever touches their carcass shall be unclean until the evening; they are unclean to you.

"And these are unclean to you among the swarming things that swarm upon the earth: the weasel, the mouse, the great lizard according to its kind, the gecko, the land crocodile, the lizard, the sand lizard, and the chameleon. These are unclean to you among all that swarm; whoever touches them when they are dead shall be unclean until the evening. And anything upon which any of them falls when they are dead shall be unclean, whether it is an article of wood or a garment or a skin or a sack, any vessel that is used for any purpose; it must be put into water, and it shall be unclean until the evening; then it shall be clean. And if any of them falls into any earthen vessel, all that is in it shall be unclean, and you shall break it. Any food in it which may be eaten, upon which water may come, shall be unclean; and all drink which may be drunk from every such vessel shall be unclean. And everything upon which any part of their carcass falls shall be unclean; whether oven or stove, it shall be broken in pieces; they are unclean, and shall be unclean to you. Nevertheless a spring or a cistern holding water shall be clean; but whatever touches their carcass shall be unclean. And if any part of their carcass falls upon any seed for sowing that is to be sown, it is clean; but if water is put on the seed and any part of their carcass falls on it, it is unclean to you.

"And if any animal of which you may eat dies, he who touches its carcass shall be unclean until the evening, and he who eats of its carcass shall wash his clothes and be unclean until the evening; he also who carries the carcass shall wash his clothes and be unclean until the evening.

"Every swarming thing that swarms upon the earth is an abomination; it shall not be eaten. Whatever goes on its belly, and whatever goes on all fours, or whatever has many feet, all the swarming things that swarm upon the earth, you shall not eat; for they are an abomination. You shall not make yourselves abominable with any swarming thing that swarms; and you shall not defile yourselves with them, lest you become unclean. For I am the Lord your God; consecrate yourselves therefore, and be holy, for I am holy. You shall not defile yourselves with any swarming thing that crawls upon the earth. For I am the Lord who brought you up out of the land of Egypt, to be your God; you shall therefore be holy, for I am holy.

This is the law pertaining to beast and bird and every living creature that moves through the waters and every creature that swarms upon the earth, to make a distinction between the unclean and the clean and between the living creature that may be eaten and the living creature that may not be eaten.

CLEAN AND UNCLEAN ANIMALS (Commentary)

Leviticus 11:1–47 (*cont'd*)

Just as chapters 1–7 served as a manual on sacrifice, so chapters 11–16 may be described as a handbook written for the priests to use on the whole question of purification. This chapter begins it by listing those beasts which are clean and those which are unclean, so therefore may be touched or not.

The very idea seems odd to us. Yet the reason for making the "distinction" (verse 47), the division, right through the animal world is no mere arbitrary whim of the Divine Being. It is Israel, the holy people, that is being addressed in this chapter: "Say to the people of Israel..." (v. 2). The uncircumcized Philistines (1 Sam. 17:36), for example, could eat what they liked; but since circumcision was the sacramental sign that a man belonged, along with his wife and children, within the holy people, he had to keep to the rules of the Covenant that God had made with Israel. He had to do so for the basic reason mentioned at verse 45: "I am the Lord your God who brought you up out of the land of Egypt, to be your God; you shall therefore be holy, as I am holy". This is what keeping the rules meant three thousand years ago. God expected Israel to be holy like himself!

But if, with the passage of time, conditions changed, then Israel must still obey, still "be holy". "Egypt" here at verse 45 stands for the disorganized, self-seeking, uncreative kind of character which may be described as unholy. God had now brought Israel out of that condition. She should not desire to live again as a slave to all the human passions from which she had been set free. But freedom is not licence. This is something that modern movements for "liberation" can learn from Leviticus: that man, under God, can be man indeed only when he serves in obedience. Man is not a mere soul living in a body. He is one whole integrated *nephesh,* to use the Hebrew word, a whole or "wholesome" person living in vital relationships with other wholesome persons. Consequently holiness must be pursued in obedience to God in a "wholesome" way; that is to say, holiness is a new way of living that affects the body as well as the mind and spirit. And this God gently invites us here to discover.

The wisdom of the ages is expressed here. Those animals which ancient man believed might carry disease (and how wise they were in most cases we are discovering only today) were therefore forbidden for food. We realize now, for example, the danger from eating undercooked pork. On the other hand, many other animals and insects are on the forbidden list here which do not seem to us to be harmful at all, such as the frogs a Frenchman enjoys or the snakes an Australian aborigine eats. B.C. man could not know that there are tropical fish which turn poisonous only for a couple of months in the year (see v. 9). But we do not expect scientific accuracy from this list, since we remember that it is God's plan to keep on revealing new depths to the meaning of holiness. And so we come in the end to Peter's dream at Acts 1:9-16; but by then he had had a new vision of holiness in the person of Jesus Christ.

The RSV lists the two varieties of animals. But we are not always sure what animals are meant in the original Hebrew. That is why other modern translations, such as the New English Bible and the Good News Bible, may suggest other creatures than the RSV. Birds of prey, of course, appear to us to be unclean, because on occasions they may eat flesh that has gone putrid. Other creatures, if handled, can infect us so that we need to wash after touching them, and even wash pots and pans that have been contaminated by them. All water containers, we read, should be kept scrupulously clean. A dead sheep in a cistern could initiate a cholera plague, as we know today. As holiness is contagious, so is unholiness. "Consecrate your-selves, therefore, and be holy, for I am holy", says the Lord (v. 44). Otherwise you cannot remain in close touch with the holy God—or with your brother man.

As we have said already, the positive content of the word

"holy" did develop over the centuries. But in that early period this conglomeration of desert folk needed the simplest and most direct instructions as to what to do and what not to do. But after another 3000 years of history we can give up drinking milk, Paul says, and start to eat strong meat for ourselves.

MATTERS OF SEX

Leviticus 12:1-8

> The Lord said to Moses, "Say to the people of Israel, If woman conceives, and bears a male child, then she shall be unclean seven days; as at the time of her menstruation, she shall be unclean. And on the eighth day the flesh of his foreskin shall be circumcised. Then she shall continue for thirty-three days in the blood of her purifying; she shall not touch any hallowed thing, nor come into the sanctuary, until the days of her purifying are completed. But if she bears a female child, then she shall be unclean two weeks, as in her menstruation; and she shall continue in the blood of her purifying for sixty-six days.
>
> "And when the days of her purifying are completed, whether for a son or for a daughter, she shall bring to the priest at the door of the tent of meeting a lamb a year old for a burnt offering, and a young pigeon or a turtledove for a sin offering, and he shall offer it before the Lord, and make atonements for her; then she shall be clean from the flow of her blood. This is the law for her who bears a child, either male or female. And if she cannot afford a lamb, then she shall take two turtledoves or two young pigeons, one for a burnt offering and the other for a sin offering; and the priest shall make atonement for her, and she shall be clean."

Let it be clear that this chapter does not suggest that sex is either unclean or unholy. The whole Bible affirms sex as God's good idea and gift to mankind, for without it the human race could not continue. The man and the woman are first attracted to each other and then united in love by means of the compelling power of sex. The Song of Songs shows us the unashamed delight of both the young man and his girl in that "whole" love which God has created and which must therefore include the body, just as, in chapter 11, we found that the "whole" person was in all aspects of living a unity of body, mind and spirit.

However, verse 2 says much more than we may think. For what does "unclean" really mean? It means "not to be touched". And so what this seemingly ancient taboo, this old ritual law, old by the time of the Second Temple, is actually telling the husband is just to be gentle and considerate to his wife. There are periods in her monthly cycle or after she has given birth when the husband must not force himself upon his wife. Marriage between two members of the Holy Nation must be seen to maintain a holy relationship. For it is possible, unfortunately, for a man to rape his own wife. Such a debased relationship is thus wholly excluded here. What is sought is a relationship of tenderness, of thoughtfulness and of reverence by the one for the other's mysterious personality. The husband must give his wife's body and psyche ample time to recover from the major and traumatic experience of childbirth which she has undergone. The period of waiting is to be forty days, not just a familiar round number that occurs many times in both Testaments, but one that echoes the forty years of cleansing that Israel underwent before she could enter the Holy Land.

So what must happen is this: a year-old lamb for a baby, whether boy or girl (they are evidently equally precious in the sight of God), is a whole offering that goes up in smoke to God. This is then followed by the offering of a pigeon, wild or tame, as a sin offering. This does not mean, as we must insist, that the act of sex with the purpose of creating a child is itself sinful. Rather, the woman is aware that all that she is and does, including having sex, is involved in her state of original sin. Consequently she asks God to let it be that her baby should be born from a *forgiven* sinner.

We have met these offerings before at 5:7–13. And we note how this divine command was obeyed in the case of the birth of Jesus (Luke 2:24). There the emphasis is laid (verse 23) on the item in the Law which says: "Every male that opens the womb shall be called holy to the Lord". No wonder the body of the mother that bore him must needs be rendered holy too.

Actually the first-born (the baby that opened the womb) was to be consecrated to God because he already belonged to God by right. "He is mine", says the Lord (Exod. 13:2).

DIAGNOSING AND DEALING WITH LEPROSY (Text)

Leviticus 13:1-59

The Lord said to Moses and Aaron, "When a man has on the skin of his body a swelling or an eruption or a spot, and it turns into a leprous disease on the skin of his body, then he shall be brought to Aaron the priest or to one of his sons the priests, and the priest shall examine the diseased spot on the skin of his body; and if the hair in the diseased spot has turned white and the disease appears to be deeper than the skin of his body, it is a leprous disease; when the priest has examined him he shall pronounce him unclean. But if the spot is white in the skin of his body, and appears no deeper than the skin, and the hair in it has not turned white, the priest shall shut up the diseased person for seven days; and the priest shall examine him on the seventh day, and if in his eyes the disease is checked and the disease has not spread in the skin, then the priest shall shut him up seven days more; and the priest shall examine him again on the seventh day, and if the diseased spot is dim and the disease has not spread in the skin, then the priest shall pronounce him clean; it is only an eruption; and he shall wash his clothes, and be clean. But if the eruption spreads in the skin, after he has shown himself to the priest for his cleansing, he shall appear again before the priest; and the priest shall make an examination, and if the eruption has spread in the skin, then the priest shall pronounce him unclean; it is leprosy.

"When a man is afflicted with leprosy, he shall be brought to the priest; and the priest shall make an examination, and if there is a white swelling in the skin, which has turned the hair white, and there is quick raw flesh in the swelling, it is a chronic leprosy in the skin of his body, and the priest shall pronounce him unclean; he shall not shut him up, for he is unclean. And if the leprosy breaks out in the skin, so that the leprosy covers all the skin of the diseased person from head to foot, so far as the priest can see, then the priest shall make an examination, and if the leprosy has covered all his body, he shall pronounce him clean of the disease; it has all turned white, and he is clean. But when raw flesh appears on him, he shall be unclean.

And the priest shall examine the raw flesh, and pronounce him unclean; raw flesh is unclean, for it is leprosy. But if the raw flesh turns again and is changed to white, then he shall come to the priest, and the priest shall examine him, and if the disease has turned white, then the priest shall pronounce the diseased person clean; he is clean.

"And when there is in the skin of one's body a boil that has healed, and in the place of the boil there comes a white swelling or a reddish-white spot, then it shall be shown to the priest; and the priest shall make an examination, and if it appears deeper than the skin and its hair has turned white, then the priest shall pronounce him unclean; it is the disease of leprosy, it has broken out in the boil. But if the priest examines it, and the hair on it is not white and it is not deeper than the skin, but is dim, then the priest shall shut him up seven days; and if it spreads in the skin, then the priest shall pronounce him unclean; it is diseased. But if the spot remains in one place and does not spread, it is the scar of the boil; and the priest shall pronounce him clean.

"Or, when the body has a burn on its skin and the raw flesh of the burn becomes a spot, reddish-white or white, the priest shall examine it, and if the hair in the spot has turned white and it appears deeper than the skin, then it is leprosy; it has broken out in the burn, and the priest shall pronounce him unclean; it is a leprous disease. But if the priest examines it, and the hair in the spot is not white and it is no deeper than the skin, but is dim, the priest shall shut him up seven days, and the priest shall examine him the seventh day; if it is spreading in the skin, then the priest shall pronounce him unclean; it is a leprous disease. But if the spot remains in one place and does not spread in the skin, but is dim, it is a swelling from the burn, and the priest shall pronounce him clean; for it is the scar of the burn.

"When a man or woman has a disease on the head or the beard, the priest shall examine the disease; and if it appears deeper than the skin, and the hair in it is yellow and thin, then the priest shall pronounce him unclean; it is an itch, a leprosy of the head or the beard. And if the priest examines the itching disease, and it appears no deeper than the skin and there is no black hair in it, then the priest shall shut up the person with the itching disease for seven days, and on the seventh day the priest shall examine the disease; and if the itch has not spread, and there is in it no yellow hair, and the itch appears to be no deeper than the skin, then he shall shave himself, but the itch he shall not shave; and the priest shall shut up the person with the itching disease for seven days more; and on the seventh day the priest shall examine the itch, and if the itch has not spread in the skin and it appears to be no deeper than the skin, then the priest shall pronounce him clean; and he shall wash his clothes, and be clean. But if the itch spreads in the skin after his cleansing, then the priest shall examine him, and if the itch has spread in the skin, the priest need not seek for the yellow hair; he is unclean. But if in his eyes the itch is checked, and black hair has grown in it, the itch is healed, he is clean; and the priest shall pronounce him clean.

"When a man or woman has spots on the skin of the body, white spots, the priest shall make an examination, and if the spots on the skin of the body are of a dull white, it is tetter that has broken out in the skin; he is clean.

"If a man's hair has fallen from his head, he is bald but he is clean. And if a man's hair has fallen from his forehead and temples, he has baldness of the forehead but he is clean. But if there is on the bald head or the bald forehead a reddish-white diseased spot, it is leprosy breaking out on his bald head or his bald forehead, like the appearance of leprosy in the skin of the body, he is a leprous man, he is unclean; the priest must pronounce him unclean; his disease is on his head.

"The leper who has the disease shall wear torn clothes and let the hair of his head hang loose, and he shall cover his upper lip and cry, 'Unclean, unclean.' He shall remain unclean as long as he has the disease; he is unclean; he shall dwell alone in a habitation outside the camp.

"When there is a leprous disease in a garment, whether a woollen or a linen garment, in warp or woof of linen or wool, or in a skin or in anything made of skin, if the disease shows greenish or reddish in the garment, whether in warp or woof or in skin or in anything made of skin, it is a leprous disease and shall be shown to the priest. And the priest shall examine the disease, and shut up that which has the disease for seven days; then he shall examine the disease on the seventh day. If the disease has spread in the garment, in warp or woof, or in the skin, the disease is a malignant leprosy; it is unclean. And he shall burn the garment, whether diseased in warp or woof, woollen or linen, or anything of skin, for it is a malignant leprosy; it shall be burned in the fire.

"And if the priest examines, and the disease has not spread in the garment in warp or woof or in anything of skin, then the priest shall command that they wash the thing in which is the disease, and he shall shut it up seven days more; and the priest shall examine the diseased thing after it has been washed. And if the diseased spot has not changed colour, though the disease has not spread, it is unclean; you shall burn it in the fire, whether the leprous spot is on the back or on the front. But if the priest examines, and the disease is dim after it is washed, he shall tear the spot out of the garment or the skin or the warp or woof; then if it appears again in the garment, in warp or woof, or in anything of skin, it is spreading; you shall burn with fire that in which is the disease. But the garment, warp or woof, or anything of skin from which the disease departs when you have washed it, shall then be washed a second time, and be clean."

This is the law for a leprous disease in a garment of wool or linen, either in warp or woof, or in anything of skin, to decide whether it is clean or unclean.

DIAGNOSING AND DEALING WITH LEPROSY
(Commentary)

Leviticus 13:1-59 (*cont'd*)

We find that in many human societies in days of old the priest was virtually the only educated man in the community; so he was expected to possess all kinds of knowledge. In old England for example, the parson was the person (meaning the only educated man) in the village. So too in Israel's case. The priest combined the offices of pastor and doctor. We notice how Jesus, in the case of the man let down through the roof (Mark 2:1–12), drew no line between the healing of the body and the healing of the soul. The theology of Jesus' position about the make-up of the human person is that which we find here in Leviticus.

The word leprosy in this chapter covers several diseases. It covers the horrible anaesthetic leprosy which exists to this day, and which destroys all feeling in the limbs. It paralyses the nerves so that the sick man can injure or burn his limb without knowing that he has done so. Then of course, all kinds of bacteria can attack the raw flesh. The word leprosy covers tuberculous leprosy also. This begins with a skin disease, but then develops into deformities (see v. 3). It covers all kinds of skin eruptions which at times evidently disappear spontane-ously (see v. 4–6). Clearly though, if the symptoms do not go away after a week's isolation, then the patient may be expected to have some form of horrifying leprosy. The chapter also includes discussion of such skin diseases as we know today under the names of ringworm, eczema, and herpes.

There has been an interesting discussion in recent years about what diseases are really included under the biblical name of leprosy. See, for example, "Leprosy and Leviticus: a Problem of Semantics and Translation", by the Rev. Dr. John Wilkin-son, *Scottish Journal of Theology,* Vol. 31, No. 2 (1978), p. 153.

In Leviticus it is recognized that certain diseases are infec-tious as well as contagious, and so the patient has to be isolated (see Job 2:7–8). A healthy person could contract the disease in question from even handling the sick man's clothing. Accor-dingly, infected clothing had to be burnt (v. 52). If it turned out that the disease after all was benign, then washing the patient's clothes was sufficient. But if it turned out to be malignant, then the patient himself had to be isolated. He was "unclean" (v. 46), and had to perform the rites of mourning as if he were dead. There was no cure in those days for infectious diseases; nor was there such at any time or in any place right up till this present century! In those days you either lived or you died! The art of medicine was confined to the healing of wounds and injuries, for which potions made from herbs and balms were evidently often quite effective.

It is the *principle* of uncleanness, however, which interests us today. Old Testament man considered himself to be a unity, as we have already emphasized. He was a whole person. This is quite a different position from that held by modern secular humanism, which stems from the philosophies of Plato and Aristotle. The Old Testament draws no line between heaven and earth, body and soul, science and religion, sport and politics, or anything else. Life is one whole, it is the "bundle of life" (1 Sam. 25:29), simply because God himself is one. The Greeks did not have one God, who is Creator and Lord of all.

So at this point we note that Leviticus cannot conceive of the body falling sick while the soul remained pure. We are aware that if you have toothache the pain can affect your temper. If you are born deformed, you may carry a chip on your shoulder all your days. If you suffer from a bad stomach you can be difficult to live with. Mussolini's autopsy, it is said, revealed that he had suffered from defective sexual organs; consequently he had compensated for this lack by wearing gaudy uniforms which he hoped would reflect his power. Hitler, a doctor reported, had only one testicle. This led, said this doctor, to his becoming a sadist. In the same way, argued Old Testament man, if you have a sick body, then you will have a sick heart. If your body is unclean, then so is your soul.

This does not mean that we are meant to think in the same way today. We must not suppose that the psychology of ancient Israel was divinely inspired! This way of thinking would not enter the head of a believing person in our society looking with compassion upon a little mongol boy or a little thalidomide girl. And yet of course there *is* sin in the situation, not the sin of the parents, but of society in general. We grasp this dimly in the case of the thalidomide baby. What this passage is saying is that there is a unity of body, mind, and spirit which was expressed in one way in Old Testament times and is expressed in a different way in ours.

Jesus believed in this unity. He said "No" to the notion, in the case of the man born blind, that either he or his parents were extra wicked (John 9). When the paralytic was let down at his feet through a hole in the roof (Mark 2:1–12), Jesus let us see that forgiving the man's sin and curing his body both reflected upon the health of the whole of his being. So what is to be emphasised is this, that it is the whole of a man's being that needs to be redeemed. This is the theme of Isa. 1:2–6 and 16–20. Only the power of God, therefore, could ever be able to do so, as we see at Num. 12:13 and 2 Kings 5:14. The great psalm of penitence, Ps. 51, asks God to do two things at once, to repair the writer's broken bones (v. 8), and to wash the whole of him, *me* (v. 2 and v. 7), in the same way as the priest in Leviticus had to deal with a man's total uncleanness, uncleanness of body and uncleanness of soul.

THE CLEANSING OF THE SICK PERSON (Text)

Leviticus 14:1–57

The Lord said to Moses, "This shall be the law of the leper for the day of his cleansing. He shall be brought to the priest; and the priest shall go out of the camp, and the priest shall make an examination. Then, if the leprous disease is healed in the leper, the priest shall command them to take for him who is to be cleansed two living clean birds and cedarwood and scarlet stuff and hyssop; and the priest shall command them to kill one of the birds in an earthen vessel over running water. He shall take the living bird with the cedarwood and the scarlet stuff and the hyssop, and dip them and the living bird in the blood of the bird that was killed over the running water; and he shall sprinkle it seven times upon him who is to be cleansed of leprosy; then he shall pronounce him clean, and shall let the living bird go into the open field. And he who is to be cleansed shall wash his clothes, and shave off all his hair, and bathe himself in water, and he shall be clean; and after that he shall come into the camp, but shall dwell outside his tent seven days. And on the seventh day he shall shave all his hair off his head; he shall shave off his beard and his eyebrows, all his hair. Then he shall wash his clothes, and bathe his body in water, and he shall be clean.

"And on the eighth day he shall take two male lambs without blemish, and one ewe lamb a year old without blemish, and a cereal offering of three tenths of an ephah of fine flour mixed with oil, and one log of oil. And the priest who cleanses him shall set the man who is to be cleansed and these things before the Lord, at the door of the tent of meeting. And the priest shall take one of the male lambs, and offer it for a guilt offering, along with the log of oil, and wave them for a wave offering before the Lord; and he shall kill the lamb in the place where they kill the sin offering and the burnt offering, in the holy place; for the guilt offering, like the sin offering, belongs to the priest; it is most holy. The priest shall take some of the blood of the guilt offering, and the priest shall put it on the tip of the right ear of him who is to be cleansed, and on the thumb of his right hand, and on the great toe of his right foot. Then the priest shall take some of the log of oil, and pour it into the palm of his own left hand, and dip his right finger in the oil that is in his left hand, and sprinkle some oil with his finger seven times before the Lord. And some of the oil that remains in his hand the priest shall put on the tip of the right ear of him who is to be cleansed, and on the thumb of his right hand, on the great toe of his right foot, upon the blood of the guilt offering; and the rest of the oil that is in the priest's hand he shall put on the head of him who is to be cleansed. Then the priest shall make atonement for him before the Lord. The priest shall offer the sin offering, to make atonement for him who is to be cleansed from his uncleanness. And afterward he shall kill the burnt offering; and the priest shall offer the burnt offering and the cereal offering on the altar. Thus the priest shall make atonement for him, and he shall be clean.

"But if he is poor and cannot afford so much, then he shall take one male lamb for a guilt offering to be waved, to make atonement for him, and a tenth of an ephah of fine flour mixed with oil for a cereal offering, and a log of oil; also two turtledoves or two young pigeons, such as he can afford; the one shall be a sin offering and the other a burnt offering. And on the eighth day he shall bring them for his cleansing to the priest, to the door of the tent of meeting, before the Lord; and the priest shall take the lamb of the guilt offering, and the log of oil, and the priest shall wave them for a wave offering before the Lord. And he shall kill the lamb of the guilt offering; and the priest shall take some of the blood of the guilt offering, and put it on the tip of the right ear of him who is to be cleansed, and on the thumb of his right hand, and on the great toe of his right foot. And the priest shall pour some of the oil into the palm of his own left hand; and shall sprinkle with his right finger some of the oil that is in his left hand seven times before the Lord; and the priest shall put some of the oil that is in his hand on the tip of the right ear of him who is to be cleansed, and on the thumb of his right hand, and the great toe of his right foot, in the place where the blood of the guilt offering was put; and the rest of the oil that is in the priest's hand he shall put on the head of him who is to be cleansed, to make atonement for him before the Lord. And he shall offer, of the turtledoves or young pigeons such as he can afford, one for a sin offering and the other for a burnt offering, along with a cereal offering; and the priest shall make atonement before the Lord for him who is being cleansed. This is the law for him in whom is a leprous disease, who cannot afford the offerings for his cleansing."

The Lord said to Moses and Aaron, "When you come into the land of Canaan, which I give you for a possession, and I put a leprous disease in a house in the land of your possession, then he who owns the house shall come and tell the priest, 'There seems to me to be some sort of disease in my house.' Then the priest shall command that they empty the house before the priest goes to examine the disease, lest all that is in the house be declared unclean; and afterward the priest shall go in to see the house. And he shall examine the disease; and if the disease is in the walls of the house with greenish or reddish spots, and if it appears to be deeper than the surface, then the priest shall go out of the house to the door of the house, and shut up the house seven days. And the priest shall come again on the seventh day, and look; and if the disease has spread in the walls of the house, then the priest shall command that they take out the stones in which is the disease and throw them into an unclean place outside the city; and he shall cause the inside of the house to be scraped round about, and the plaster that they scrape off they shall pour into an unclean place outside the city; then they shall take other stones and put them in the place of those stones, and he shall take other plaster and plaster the house.

"If the disease breaks out again in the house, after he has taken out the stones and scraped the house and plastered it, then the priest shall go and look; and if the disease has spread in the house, it is a malignant leprosy in the house; it is unclean. And he shall break down the house, its stones and timber and all the plaster of the house; and he shall carry them forth out of the city to an unclean place. Moreover he who enters the house while it is shut up shall be unclean until the evening; and he who lies down in the house shall wash his clothes; and he who eats in the house shall wash his clothes.

"But if the priest comes and makes an examination, and the disease has not spread in the house after the house was plastered, then the priest shall pronounce the house clean, for the disease is healed. And for the cleansing of the house he shall take two small birds, with cedarwood and scarlet stuff and hyssop, and shall kill one of the birds in an earthen vessel over running water, and shall take the cedarwood and the hyssop and the scarlet stuff, along with the living bird, and dip them in the blood of the bird that was killed and in the running water, and sprinkle the house seven times. Thus he shall cleanse the house with the blood of the bird, and with the running water, and with the living bird, and with the cedarwood and hyssop and scarlet stuff; and he shall let the living bird go out of the city into the open field; so he shall make atonement for the house, and it shall be clean."

This is the law for any leprous disease: for an itch, for leprosy in a garment or in a house, and for a swelling or an eruption or a spot, to show when it is unclean and when it is clean. This is the law for leprosy.

THE CLEANSING OF THE SICK PERSON
(Commentary)

Leviticus 14:1-57 (*cont'd*)

The actions here are significant. The sick man or woman (or child) must go to the priest, for he alone knows the mind of God. The priest must then examine the patient *outside the camp* (v. 3), that is to say, away from the "holy place". Evidently the patient must not contaminate the place where a man meets with the Holy God. And yet the priest is to be lovingly willing to handle the poor leper. But the patient may return into the community and become part of the holy people again if he appears to be cured, and the priest has performed the necessary sacrifice, and let the people *see* that God has forgiven him. At it the shedding of blood is required again.

After this sacrifice a living creature, a bird that has been dipped in the sacrificial blood, is set free to be a kind of scape-goat that carries the evil thing away from human habitation. The function of this bird is not to be compared with that of the scape-goat we meet with in chapter 16. Then a second bird is required, one that has been sacrificed over *living* water (as is the Hebrew for "running"). It becomes the means of sprinkling the patient with the sacrificial blood. We recall that *blood poured forth* is the symbol of *life* poured out. Finally the patient himself must go through the prescribed ritual of cleansing.

This sacrifice is called an *asham*. Note how it is made up. The animal for the *asham* is never substituted for by a less expensive offering if the offerer turns out to be too poor (v. 21). It is not commutable to a silver offering as is the ordinary *asham,* since the blood of the lamb is needed for the prescribed ritual (v. 14, v. 25). As against the other rituals which we have now observed, this *asham* takes precedence over all other sacrifices and is the first to be offered up during the ritual of the eighth day (v. 23). The leper's *asham,* moreover, is the only sacrifice found in Leviticus to include the wave offering. This places it on a high pedestal of importance. It is with the blood of the lamb that the leper is daubed, and not with any other sacrificial animal.

Before this the leper had to be isolated and had to live alone and be a pariah. So his isolation was now a living picture of that terrible state of which we say today: "Hell is total isolation". But into this "hellish" situation comes the redemptive power of the living God. The *asham* is performed "before the Lord" (v. 12, v. 16), and at the command of the Lord (v. 1). Moreover, because the action is of God, it is bound to be effective; therefore *he shall be clean* (v. 20). The *asham* is effective even for the poorest of the poor. It is *always* a lamb that is slain to conclude this ritual, whatever else is used as well. It is the *blood* of the lamb that, at the Word of the Lord, renders the redemption effective, so that the leper is cleansed (1 John 1:9 takes up this word "cleansed") from top to toe (v. 25). Thus as a sign of this total cleansing the new life of forgiveness and health is applied actually to the stricken body of the poor leper, from top to toe (vv. 28–29).

THE MYSTERY OF EVIL

Just as no man is an island unto himself, so it is with the evil in the world. The mystery of evil cannot be dissociated even from the purposes of God. For it is God who puts the disease of leprosy in a man's home (v. 33)! Clearly many a human being would never come to recognize that he is a sinner who needs the cleansing of his soul unless God had first awakened him to the discovery that his body needs it too.

> See now that I, even I, am he,
>   and there is no god beside me;

I kill and I make alive;
    I wound and I heal;
And there is none that can deliver out of my hand!

                            (Deut. 32:39)

That verse was spoken several centuries before our present chapter in Leviticus was penned. So this had been the faith of Israel for many generations already!

Diseases, like human sin, may be infectious, and may be conveyed by inanimate objects. Even the walls of a house may need cleansing. Thus they may need to be washed with "scarlet stuff" (the colour of blood) and with hyssop, a pungent, aromatic plant (v. 49). In this case, too, blood was needed (v. 52) along with pure, clean running water, and cedarwood, the wood from which the Tabernacle was built; and once again a living bird, covered with blood, was set free to return to the living God. So the little creature bore the blood of the sacrifice right up to the heart of God. We are thus reminded that it is not only man who is a fallen creature needing to be redeemed. So is his environment! This fact is not appreciated by those today who declare that if only individuals are converted to God, all else will fall into place. The procedure for "fumigating" a house is here shown to be exactly the same as that used for cleansing a skin disease in a human being. All nature is one, and man's body is of the earth, earthy (Gen. 2:7).

Psalm 51 can use the same language about a man's soul that is employed for environmental cleansing. "Purge me with hyssop, and I shall be clean; wash me, and I shall be whiter than snow" (Ps. 51:7). God is not merely the redeemer of "souls", he is the redeemer of the whole earth. At the present time the whole creation is groaning in travail (Rom. 8:22) waiting to be redeemed. But the God of redemption has planned to make from it "new heavens and a new earth" (Isa. 66:22; Rev. 21:1)— a new world of both matter and spirit; in other words, not a heaven of immortal souls, but a resurrection, a re-creation of all things.

HOLINESS MEANS CLEANLINESS (Text)

Leviticus 15:1–33

The Lord said to Moses and Aaron, "Say to the people of Israel, When any man has a discharge from his body, his discharge is unclean. And this is the law of his uncleanness for a discharge: whether his body runs with his discharge, or his body is stopped from discharge, it is uncleanness in him. Every bed on which he who has the discharge lies shall be unclean; and everything on which he sits shall be unclean. And any one who touches his bed shall wash his clothes, and bathe himself in water, and be unclean until the evening. And whoever sits on anything on which he who has the discharge has sat shall wash his clothes, and bathe himself in water, and be unclean until the evening. And whoever touches the body of him who has the discharge shall wash his clothes, and bathe himself in water, and be unclean until the evening. And if he who has the discharge spits on one who is clean, then he shall wash his clothes, and bathe himself in water, and be unclean until the evening. And any saddle on which he who has the discharge rides shall be unclean. And whoever touches anything that was under him shall be unclean until the evening; and he who carries such a thing shall wash his clothes, and bathe himself in water, and be unclean until the evening. Any one whom he that has the discharge touches without having rinsed his hands in water shall wash his clothes, and bathe himself in water, and be unclean until the evening. And the earthen vessel which he who has the discharge touches shall be broken; and every vessel of wood shall be rinsed in water.

"And when he who has a discharge is cleansed of his discharge, then he shall count for himself seven days for his cleansing, and wash his clothes; and he shall bathe his body in running water, and shall be clean. And on the eighth day he shall take two turtledoves or two young pigeons, and come before the Lord to the door of the tent of meeting, and give them to the priest; and the priest shall offer them, one for a sin offering and the other for a burnt offering; and the priest shall make atonement for him before the Lord for his discharge.

"And if a man has an emission of semen, he shall bathe his whole body in water, and be unclean until the evening. And every garment and every skin on which the semen comes shall be washed with water, and be unclean until the evening. If a man lies with a woman and has an emission of semen, both of them shall bathe themselves in water, and be unclean until the evening.

"When a woman has a discharge of blood which is her regular discharge from her body, she shall be in her impurity for seven days, and whoever touches her shall be unclean until the evening. And everything upon which she lies during her impurity shall be unclean; everything also upon which she sits shall be unclean. And whoever touches her bed shall wash his clothes, and bathe himself in water, and be unclean until the evening. And whoever touches anything upon which she sits shall wash his clothes, and bathe himself in water, and be unclean until the evening; whether it is the bed or anything upon which she sits, when he touches it he shall be unclean until the evening. And if any man lies with her, and her impurity is on him, he shall be unclean seven days; and every bed on which he lies shall be unclean.

"If a woman has a discharge of blood for many days, not at the time of her impurity, or if she has a discharge beyond the time of her impurity, all the days of the discharge she shall continue in uncleanness; as in the days of her impurity, she shall be unclean. Every bed on which she lies, all the days of her discharge, shall be to her as the bed of her impurity; and everything on which she sits shall be unclean, as in the uncleanness of her impurity. And whoever touches these things shall be unclean, and shall wash his clothes, and bathe himself in water, and be unclean until the evening. But if she is cleansed of her discharge, she shall count for herself seven days, and after that she shall be clean. And on the eighth day she shall take two turtledoves or two young pigeons, and bring them to the priest, to the door of the tent of meeting. And the priest shall offer one for a sin offering and the other for a burnt offering; and the priest shall make atonement for her before the Lord for her unclean discharge.

"Thus you shall keep the people of Israel separate from their uncleanness, lest they die in their uncleanness by defiling my tabernacle that is in their midst."

This is the law for him who has a discharge and for him who has an emission of semen, becoming unclean thereby; also for her who is sick with her impurity; that is, for any one, male or female, who has a discharge, and for the man who lies with a woman who is unclean.

HOLINESS MEANS CLEANLINESS (Commentary)

Leviticus 15:1–33 (*cont'd*)

In this chapter we find that the priest is not only doctor but also pastor to the individual families of Israel. His task is not confined to matters connected with public worship. He has to enter even the intimacies of the home. His is the duty to teach the rich and the poor, educated and uneducated alike, some simple rules of hygiene, including some facts about infection and how to deal with it.

It is notable that in the Middle Ages, when, on a number of occasions, up to a third of the population of Europe's cities perished from the plague which they called the Black Death, Jews, though living in the confined areas of the ghettos of those same cities, suffered from the plague to a much lesser extent than did their fellow-citizens. In their bewilderment, therefore, there were those who declared that since the Jews "were not dying like flies as we Gentiles are", clearly the devil must be looking after his own. Such ignorant and biased persons added fuel to the fires of the latent anti-Semitism of the times, and continued to arouse the bereaved citizens to take vengeance on those "enemies of Christ", the Jews. But the near immunity of the Jew from infection in reality sprang from the fact that he kept strictly the laws on hygiene that we find in our book of Leviticus, now developed somewhat in a treatise in the Talmud.

We are told in 2 Sam. 11:4 that the heinousness of David's lust for the body of Bathsheba was compounded by the fact that she was "purifying herself from her uncleanness". It is this practice that is referred to here. Viscount Melbourne, who died in 1848, and so was a true Victorian, once declared: "Things have come to a pretty pass when religion is allowed to invade the sphere of private life." But verses 13–14 reveal how "religion" does come right into a man's very personal habits. This "infringement of his personal rights" by God himself extended to cover even the sexual practices that unite a man and his wife (v. 24). So sex matters and personal cleanliness come together here.

We find guidance even for the living of married life in these prescriptions. For example, verse 16 implies that the husband should realize there are times when he should abstain from intercourse, or that having intercourse once in twenty-four hours should suffice. Verse 19 implies that a woman's menstrual period is to be respected; and verse 25 insists on there being no intercourse at all if the woman is unwell. So again we meet with suggestions about tenderness, affection and self-control in the married state, and the need by the male to respect the rhythmical cycle of a woman's sexual being; he should never force himself upon her when he alone desires to have intercourse.

The basic reason for all these regulations, as noted at verse 31, is that uncleanness is an offence against the beautiful mystery of the human body which God has created and which he has given to us as a holy thing. As St. Paul declares, "Your body is a temple of the Holy Spirit within you" (1 Cor. 6:19). Consequently, just like any other offence against our neighbour, sexual impurity can infect our neighbour only too easily (v. 8). And that is a sin against love. What of the influence of television today?

If we tread the precincts of "*my* Tabernacle", the holy place, says God (and for us today even the kitchen and the stable can be holy places, as we have already noted from Zech. 14:20–21), then, in our uncleanness we actually pollute the holiness of God. Then there is nothing we can do to *un*do our blind stumbling except to obey and do in faith what God himself has told us to do. As Paul in Rom. 12:1 puts it, to those who now see the sacrificial commands of Leviticus in the light of the sacrifice of Christ: "I appeal to you therefore, brethren, by the mercies of God, to present your bodies as a living sacrifice, *holy* and acceptable to God, which is your spiritual worship."

THE DAY OF ATONEMENT (Text)

Leviticus 16:1–34

The Lord spoke to Moses, after the death of the two sons of Aaron, when they drew near before the Lord and died; and the Lord said to Moses, "Tell Aaron your brother not to come at all times into the holy place within the veil, before the mercy seat which is upon the ark, lest he die; for I will appear in the cloud upon the mercy seat. But thus shall Aaron come into the holy place: with a young bull for a sin offering and a ram for a burnt offering. He shall put on the holy linen coat, and shall have the linen breeches on his body, be girded with the linen girdle, and wear the linen turban; these are the holy garments. He shall bathe his body in water, and then put them on. And he shall take from the congregation of the people of Israel two male goats for a sin offering, and one ram for a burnt offering.

"And Aaron shall offer the bull as a sin offering for himself, and shall make atonement for himself and for his house. Then he shall take the two goats, and set them before the Lord at the door of the tent of meeting; and Aaron shall cast lots upon the two goats, one lot for the Lord and the other lot for Azazel. And Aaron shall present the goat on which the lot fell for the Lord, and offer it as a sin offering; but the goat on which the lot fell for Azazel shall be presented alive before the Lord to make atonement over it, that it may be sent away into the wilderness to Azazel.

"Aaron shall present the bull as a sin offering for himself, and shall make atonement for himself and for his house; he shall kill the bull as a sin offering for himself. And he shall take a censer full of coals of fire from the altar before the Lord, and two handfuls of sweet incense beaten small; and he shall bring it within the veil and put the incense on the fire before the Lord, that the cloud of the incense may cover the mercy seat which is upon the testimony, lest he die; and he shall take some of the blood of the bull, and sprinkle it with his finger on the front of the mercy seat, and before the mercy seat he shall sprinkle the blood with his finger seven times.

"Then he shall kill the goat of the sin offering which is for the people, and bring its blood within the veil, and do with its blood as he did with the blood of the bull, sprinkling it upon the mercy seat and before the mercy seat; thus he shall make atonement for the holy place, because of the uncleannesses of the people of Israel, and because of their transgressions, all their sins; and so he shall do for the tent of meeting, which abides with them in the midst of their uncleannesses. There shall be no man in the tent of meeting when he enters to make atonement in the holy place until he comes out and has made atonement for himself and for his house and for all the assembly of Israel. Then he shall go out to the altar which is before the Lord and make atonement for it, and shall take some of the blood of the bull and of the blood of the goat, and put it on the horns of the altar round about. And he shall sprinkle some of the blood upon it with his finger seven times, and cleanse it and hallow it from the uncleannesses of the people of Israel.

"And when he has made an end of atoning for the holy place and the tent of meeting and the altar, he shall present the live goat; and Aaron shall lay both his hands upon the head of the live goat, and confess over him all the iniquities of the people of Israel, and all their transgressions, all their sins; and he shall put them upon the head of the goat, and send him away into the wilderness by the hand of a man who is in readiness. The goat shall bear all their iniquities upon him to a solitary land; and he shall let the goat go into the wilderness.

"Then Aaron shall come into the tent of meeting, and shall put off the linen garments which he put on when he went into the holy place, and shall leave them there; and he shall bathe his body in water in a holy place, and put on his garments, and come forth, and offer his burnt offering and the burnt offering of the people, and make atonement for himself and for the people. And the fat of the sin offering he shall burn upon the altar. And he who lets the goat go to Azazel shall wash his clothes and bathe his body in water, and afterward he may come into the camp. And the bull for the sin offering and the goat for the sin offering, whose blood was brought in to make atonement in the holy place, shall be carried forth outside the camp; their skin and their flesh and their dung shall be burned with fire. And he who burns them shall wash his clothes and bathe his body in water, and afterward he may come into the camp.

"And it shall be a statute to you for ever that in the seventh month, on the tenth day of the month, you shall afflict yourselves, and shall do no work, either the native or the stranger who sojourns among you; for on this day shall atonement be made for you, to cleanse you; from all your sins you shall be clean before the Lord. It is a sabbath of solemn rest to you, and you shall afflict yourselves; it is a statute for ever. And the priest who is anointed and consecrated as priest in his father's place shall make atonement, wearing the holy linen garments; he shall make atonement for the sanctuary, and he shall make atonement for the tent of meeting and for the altar, and he shall make atonement for the priests and for all the people of the assembly. And this shall be an everlasting statute for you, that atonement may be made for the people of Israel once in the year because of all their sins." And Moses did as the Lord commanded him.

THE DAY OF ATONEMENT (Commentary)

Leviticus 16:1–34 (*cont'd*)

Chapters 11–15, which we have now studied, consist of a block of material containing regulations on uncleanness. Now, at chapter 16, we continue from where chapter 10 left off, to learn about the most important of all the regulations found in the Law of Moses—what is to be done on the Day of Atonement (it is given this name only at 23:27–28), and what it is all about. At the same time it is the supreme act of cleansing and therefore appropriately described at this point.

We find no mention of that great day in any of the historical books of the Old Testament. Yet the nucleus of the complicated ritual which we meet with here must have been in existence from quite early days. It was only after the return from exile, that is to say, towards the end of the sixth century B.C., that the ritual we meet with here flowered in all its fullness of detail. In other words, the ritual of the Day of Atonement grew and developed as the need for all the elements in it grew in parallel with Israel's awareness of God's grace and forgiving love. In much the same way, the Church's actions connected with the sacrament of Holy Communion grew and developed from the simple actions of Christ which we find in the story of the Last Supper until we come to the elaborate ritual of a High Mass today.

Parallel with the development of this ritual here we note that the number of holocausts, of *'olahs,* which we met in previous chapters, seems also to have grown and grown. In consequence, by Jesus' day there was an almost continual column of smoke going up from the altar in the Temple, and the smell of blood and of scores of animal carcasses must have been quite nauseating to many citizens. That was why, even as early on as the dedication of the Second Temple in 515 B.C., thoughtful people were beginning to ask this basic question: If these burnt offerings are meant to obtain God's forgiveness for our sins, then must they really go on, and on, and on? Why should they need to be repeated at all? Does God not forgive sinners in Israel once and for all, and does he not accept the atoning sacrifice as being complete in itself?

It is from this chapter again that the ritual for *Yom Kippur,* followed once a year in every Jewish synagogue ever since the destruction of the Temple in A.D. 70 till the present day, has been developed. *Yom* means Day; *Kippur* means Atonement. But just what does the word "atonement" really mean now that it is no longer possible to sacrifice animals in a synagogue, although this has been specifically enjoined at 23:27?

We note that it was not a mere functionary who carried out the ritual for this special day. It was our very human Aaron, a man who had suffered the agony of witnessing the disobedience of his own two sons (10:1–3), to be followed by the horror of watching the righteous judgment of God fall upon them. We read at 10:3 that "Aaron held his peace". Poor man. He had suffered hell, yet he evidently still clung to his faith. The result of the sin of his sons, moreover, had in a sense infected their father, just as leprosy spreads from one person to another. Aaron could no longer go in and come out of the holy place at will (v. 2).

In the holy place there rested "the mercy seat which is upon the ark" (v. 2). This was not a seat at all. It was a "place", "a place with a purpose". Over the ark two fabricated cherubs spread their wings, fashioned so that their wing tips just met over the middle of this "box" (Exod. 25:17–21). Inside the ark, which was much the size of a coffin, there rested the tablets of the Law (Deut. 10:5). It was actually *there,* at that point where holiness and righteousness met (see again Isa. 5:16), where the unspeakable majesty and "otherness" of God fused with his saving love (as the word "righteousness" develops to mean), that the *mercy* of God was to be found. What a tremendous conception! And what a terrible revelation of the mystery of God's forgiving love, coming as it did "out of the cloud" (v. 2) which veiled the awe-fulness of the living God from the eyes of man! This whole series of symbols is beautifully described at Exod. 40:34-38.

"Mercy seat" is actually only one word, *kapporeth*. Thus there is not even a word for "seat" in the Hebrew. It was Martin Luther, 450 years ago, who invented the phrase "mercy seat" when he made his famous translation of the Bible into German. *Kapporeth* really means "covering". It was not a "thing" at all, but it was the place where God's holy love covered the sinner and so hid him from the judgment he certainly deserved. (See Exod. 25:17-22 for a description.) It did not cover his "sin", however, and thus make it invisible to God. That is not possible. For there is no such thing as sin without a sinner. "Sin" is only the symptom of a diseased personality. The *kapporeth* covered the *sinner*.

Accordingly, since the sinner in Israel had now been made aware of all this, over the years he had grown progressively dissatisfied with sacrifices that dealt merely with specific sins and individual uncleannesses. What his soul longed for was a sacramental act that could deal with *him* as a sinner, one which would really put him right with God, there and then, *once and for all*. This is what the ritual of the Day of Atonement aimed to do.

THE RITUAL FOR THE DAY

Leviticus 16:1-34 *(cont'd)*

We remember that the name Aaron (v. 2-3) came to signify the later High Priest of historical times. The High Priest, then, had first to make *himself* "holy" if he were to dare to approach the holy place (v. 3-6). This ritual is described at Exod. 29:1-36. For the ornate vestments he wore on this occasion see Exod. 28.

Verses 6-10 offer a short summary of the main ritual which is described in detail in the rest of the chapter. What then was the High Priest to do?

(1) He first had to offer a bull and a ram for his own sin—not individual sins!—but for his very alienation of heart and mind

from God. Not only so, but since he was also a family man, he was to make atonement for his wife and children as well. No man is an island unto himself, we say today. The verb "to make atonement" (*kipper*) describes an actual action. In the same way, the New Testament insists that Christ's death on the Cross was not a passive acceptance of the forces of evil; it was a deliberate *action* on Jesus' part in obedience to the will of God.

(2) The vestments he put on for the celebration were not his high priestly ones. On this one day in the year, when he did the holiest thing of all, he was to wear the vestments of any ordinary priest.

(3) He was to bring two goats to the entrance to the holy place. Having cast lots, he selected one of the two goats "for the Lord", while the other was set aside "for Azazel".

(4) The goat for the Lord he literally "made it into sin". It is from an expression such as this that St. Paul takes his theology when he declares at 2 Cor. 5:21: "For our sake he [God] made him [Jesus] to be sin who knew no sin, so that in him [cf. laying one's hand on the head of the sacrificial animal to identify oneself with it] we might become the righteousness of God [that is, actually become the instrument of God's saving love which is transferred to us at the 'mercy seat']."

(5) The goat "for Azazel" was not sacrificed, though it was "presented alive before the Lord to make atonement over it".

(6) Meanwhile God's real presence was made available above the mercy seat (see v. 2). Because of this the High Priest had to make sure that the holy place was filled with the smoke of the incense, so that God should remain invisible to the eye of sinful man. For "no man shall see God and live" (Exod. 33:20). Then he had to sprinkle some of the blood from his own bull seven times, not *upon* (that would be too dangerous now) but *in front of* the mercy seat. The reason for this action was that God had made a vital concession to Israel by consenting to dwell amidst the impurities endemic to our ordinary human life together. So God required that the *place* where he made himself to be known should be "cleaned up" before the great action could take place. It is the *place* that is sanctified here, and not

the people! They are mentioned only at the tail-end of verse 33. Yet why is all this to take place? The answer comes fair and square: "For I am holy, says the Lord."

(7) Having killed the people's goat, the High Priest had to make many ritual acts with its blood—sprinkling the *mercy seat* to make atonement for sinful Israel, then the *holy place,* and then the *altar.* During these actions he alone was allowed to enter the *Tent of Meeting,* and his entrance formed the focal point of the whole series of activities. He thus acted as *representative* of the people when he went through the *veil,* the curtain of the holy place, *right into the real presence of the living God.* Yet we must note in passing that, despite this great annual event, the individual sinner was never shut out from receiving forgiveness if by chance there was no priest available. He could approach God and receive forgiveness anywhere and at any time. See 1 Sam. 7:6; 1 Kings 8:33–43; Ezra 10:1; Neh. 1:6; 9:31.

(8) Then the High Priest presented *the live goat.* With the laying on of hands, accompanied by a prayer of confession, by which the priest revealed what those sins really are, the iniquities of the people were placed on the head of the goat. Then a layman led the goat away from the Tabernacle (or later in history, from the Temple) into the wilderness, the area where no man lived, and let the beast run free. This goat was "the goat for Azazel" mentioned at verses 8 and 10.

(9) Finally, he had to "defuse" the tension of the whole drama. He was to "disinfect" himself, and wash off from his clothes and his body the contact he had had with the "holy", and make a sacrifice for the same purpose for the people too. Even the goat-herd was to wash himself as well. The carcass of the bull whose blood was used at verse 15, as well as that of the first goat, were to be removed from all contact with the "holy" and burnt "outside the camp". In fact, even those who dragged the beasts away had also to perform a ritual purification.

(10) This Day of Atonement was to be made an annual event (v. 29). The date of it was fixed, and to this day it occurs towards the end of September. It even became an extra Sabbath, when

no work of any kind was done. "You shall afflict yourselves on it." And so it became something like the Ash Wednesday of our Christian calendar.

WHAT THE DAY OF ATONEMENT IS ALL ABOUT

Leviticus 16:1–34 (*cont'd*)

There are two issues to look at, both of which have great theological significance.

Once and for all. We said earlier that the growing hope and despair of the Hebrew people, tired of so many sacrifices in their life, was for just one act of sacrifice that would, *once and for all,* assure them of the forgiveness of God. And we have also seen that that was exactly why the ritual of the Day of Atonement was finally established in all the detail we have here after the return of the people from exile. And yet—the people's hopes had not been really met after all. The Day of Atonement was indeed to take place once a year (v. 34) at the command of God, and this, of course, was a great advance in the direction they were longing for. On the other hand, it was not enough.

The Letter to the Hebrews in the New Testament is intensely interested in the ceremonies attached to the Day of Atonement. All we can say here, of course, is that its writer claims that Christ is the Church's High Priest, and that he alone has entered within the veil and seen God face to face; and that he has brought the blood of the lamb into God's real presence. Moreover, it declares, he has done so now in reality *once and for all* (*eph hapax*), so that his action need never be repeated (Heb. 8–10). For Christ, says the writer, made himself into the *asham* that has now taken away the sins of the world. This chapter in Leviticus is a clear case of a book in the Old Testament presenting us with a definitive interpretation of an aspect of New Testament theology.

The Goat for Azazel. No one knows where this name comes from or what it means. That however is not so important as to know what the goat was meant to do. It carried off the sin of the people into the wilderness.

A glance at a map of Palestine reveals that the "Wilderness of Judea" lies only a few miles away from Jerusalem, on the eastern slope of the main divide, and extending right down to the Dead Sea. The rain-bearing winds from the Mediterranean never reach this area. This wilderness is where both John the Baptist and Jesus each remained for a period. It was the haunt of jackals and the "night-hag" (whatever that was), of demons and evil spirits; and Azazel was one of those jinns or demons. (Islam accepts their existence literally. See *The Qoran, Sura,* or chapter 72. Mohammed believed in their existence, but condemned the worship of them.) It is difficult for modern, sophisticated man to realize that Europe only began to shake off its horror of ghosties and things that go bump in the night a couple of hundred years or so ago, or to be sympathetic with folk of other cultures who still hold the inhabitants of a wilderness in dread.

But what was the point of sending off the people's sins into the wilderness? The action taught Israel a basically important fact about the nature of God. The sacrifice of the one goat "for the Lord" assured the worshipper that God does indeed forgive sins. But forgiveness does not conclude the matter. The effect of our sins remains even when we have been forgiven. God may forgive us even if we kill a man. But God's forgiveness does not bring the dead man back to life. A parent may be forgiven for actual cruelty to his child, but the child may carry the scar of that cruelty on his soul to the end of his days. The result of sin *remains*. It is still there as part of God's universe. God may cast the sin behind his back (Isa. 38:17)—*but its effect is still there*. The idea that sin is not really important, because God can forgive the sinner, is not a biblical idea. Israel used to speak of the Wilderness of Judea as being "behind God's back" (where the goat for Azazel was sent). But it still represents that mystery of *chaos* which was there in the beginning when God began to create the heavens and the earth (see the footnote to Gen. 1:1 in the RSV). That chaos is still with us today, even though it is still behind God's back.

TEN THEOLOGICAL INSIGHTS TO DATE

We have now reached the end of the first part of Leviticus. We might therefore look back to see what God has been saying, not just to ancient Israel but also to us, in these 16 chapters. Yet, for obvious reasons, we can select only a few highlights.

(1) We have noticed to date that each new section in our book is introduced by a phrase such as "The Lord *said* to Moses...". Speech comes out of the mouth only of a living person. No wonder therefore that the Old Testament refers to God emphatically as *the living God,* for he is wholly unlike the gods of the nations. There is no discussion in our book about the existence of God. How can you even raise such a question when you have heard him "speak" in his mighty act of rescuing you and "bringing you up out of the land of Egypt" (11:45)?

(2) The *Word* of God, having come from the living, creative, redeeming God, *gets things done.* God's Word is effective. It must be such, of course, since it comes from *God.* Thus when God says "...then you will be forgiven", you *are,* in fact, forgiven. Leviticus tells how Israelites received an *assurance* of God's love and loyalty and re-creative power in their lives.

(3) God's forgiveness was a *fact.* These narratives are not a foretelling of what God would do centuries later in Christ. They were not a prophecy of the future. A book like Leviticus helps the Christian to realize that the Old Testament is indeed the *Holy Scripture* to which the New Testament refers. It is *the* Bible (Rom. 1:2). Leviticus opens up to us the depths of the amazing Christology (the theology about Christ) that we meet with in John's Gospel and in Paul's Letter to the Colossians, the latter especially at 1:15-20. At John 8:58, for example, we read the words: "Before Abraham was, I am." At Rev. 1:4, the living Christ is he "who is and who was and who is to come". These New Testament writers thus stress that the redemptive work of Christ which he *did* in A.D. 33 is effective for the salvation of the world not just from that date onwards till our present day, but backwards also to the time "before Abraham was". John 1:1-4

declares that Christ was that very same Word which brought forgiveness to Israel (Lev. 4:20, etc.).

Leviticus therefore clarifies for us the great New Testament assertions that Christ is not the mere adopted Son of God, but that "in him all things were created" (Col. 1:16); and that since Christ is the "head" of the Church, or the Church is the "body" of Christ, then the Church is no late comer into the world, nor is it merely two thousand years old. Because Christ himself is eternal, his "body" too has been there since before Abraham was, so that, as Gen. 4:26 puts this truth, not in a historical, but in a theological statement of fact. Right from the beginning men have called upon the *Name* of the Lord.

(4) Forgiveness is not something that God does by a mere wave of the hand. Forgiveness is *costly*—to God. It is obtained only by the shedding of blood, and blood is life itself. This point is made scores of times in Leviticus. Therefore it is basic to our understanding of how God works in the world. God has chosen to work by crises:

> I kill and I make alive;
> I wound and I heal (Deut. 32:39).

In the Old Testament the prophets declare that God's "plan", his *'etsah,* for his world does not go forward in smooth development. "Things are getting better and better", we may say; or "We shall build Jerusalem in England's green and pleasant land." No, says the whole Old Testament. God's *'etsah* works through pain and suffering. Don't listen, Jesus said, when men say "Lo, here is the Kingdom of God, lo there". One of the satanic temptations Jesus underwent at the beginning of his ministry was to accept the innuendo that his task was merely to preach the Gospel, heal the sick, feed the hungry, but at the same time to turn his back on the book of Leviticus. That temptation climaxed for him in the Garden of Gethsemane. He was then only thirty-three years old. His agony arose from this—surely God could give him another thirty-three years to bring to this warring, greedy and lost world the good news of God's redeeming love before it was too late! In fact, so ran his temptation, how could such *not* be God's will for him? Surely he had only just begun his ministry?

But God had already spoken in Leviticus. The historical fact is that the way of merely preaching and teaching did actually fail that very evening, for "they all ran away and left him" (Matt. 26:56). This is because there is only one way, God's revealed way, the way of sacrifice and the shedding of blood. And on that night Jesus accepted it. Yet even in his agony of mind he took time to say: "Watch and pray that you may not enter into *this temptation that I am facing now"* (Matt. 26:41). Surely that is a word spoken to us today!

(5) God is *holy*. His holiness is revealed as his compassionate, saving love right in the midst of his people. God is not only transcendent that is, utterly beyond human thought, he is also immanent (to use the theological term), which in Hebrew is *Immanuel*, or "God is here with us".

(6) There is a divine purpose and plan working out through all the legislation found in Leviticus. Its aim is that Israel might *live* (and not die like Nadab and Abihu in chapter 10). What is it that leads to death? It is alienation from God through disobedience to his Word, or through refusing to believe that alienation from one's fellows is brought about by actions such as adultery. This is just what Jesus affirmed too. "I came that they may have life, and have it abundantly" (John 10:10).

(7) The Israel with whom God works is chosen, and this is made evident by the very fact that she has been rescued from a living death. Lev. 11:45 echoes the terms of God's covenant with Israel which we read at Exod. 19:5-6. There Israel is to be holy even as God is holy, and so to be "a kingdom of priests". The charge given to a priest is that he should be responsible for his flock, not merely for himself. Israel is to be God's priestly instrument to the nations of the world. Israel has been *chosen to serve*. As Jesus puts it: "Many are called". There are lots of simple, believing people, like the centurion who came to Jesus in faith, asking him to restore his servant to health. "But few are chosen", adds Jesus. Only some believers are selected and trained by God, not in order to be saved—heaven forbid!—but

so as to be God's special instruments of his redeeming love for all mankind. To reject *that* calling is more terrible than never to have known of God's love at all.

(8) God uses intermediaries. He uses the High Priest as his instrument to convey his forgiveness at the Day of Atonement. He uses the whole body of priests to convey his Word to the ordinary man. He trains all Israel (as families) to be his kingdom of priests to the peoples of the world.

(9) Israel can be this instrument only if all members of that people respect and love each other and so uphold the moral law which God has revealed as the foundation of their very reason for existence.

(10) All is of *grace.* Israel exists only because God acted first. He rescued Israel out of Egypt, gave her a land on which she could stand upright and look him in the eye, so to speak. Every child born into Israel was an heir to this primary act of God's grace. The sign for that was that on the eighth day the baby boy was circumcized (12:3). Thereafter he could use the various "means of grace" listed in Leviticus to keep him from being separated from the People of God. In the same way, then, Paul declares that Christ died for us while we were yet sinners. That is grace indeed! So we baptize the infant boy (*or girl*—for in Christ there is neither male nor female), and he is then a member of the rescued "congregation" (4:13). Thereafter God's gifts of the various means of grace are there to keep him from falling out of the Kingdom. It was not his decision that he was called to serve, it was God's grace that made it happen (John 15:16). The baptized child is thus a Christian child. The renegade adult member of the *congregation* may have become an apostate, and thus fall truly under the judgment of God (Matt. 18:3). But he who lives by the Word of God need never be afraid.

THE HOLINESS CODE

Leviticus chapters 17–26 go by that name. Together they form what we might call part 2 of our book. These chapters are clearly a separate unit, a separate little book. They form a compilation of laws all of which have to do with the key idea of "Be holy, for I am holy, says the Lord."

THE MEANING OF THE WORD "HOLY"

In early days the word "holy" meant something like *taboo,* a Polynesian word meaning "Don't touch—or you will be in trouble!" In many parts of the world people considered that the Divine Being must never be antagonized, or he might hit out in anger. Wherever you look—in Africa, Arabia, Australia—you find holy places, holy because the divinity of the place dwelled there. So it is that when Moses' attention was attracted to the Burning Bush (Exod. 3:1-6), and he started to go forward to find out what this curious sight was, he heard a voice say, "Don't come near; take off your shoes, for you are on holy ground."

Isaiah, more than anyone else, put real meaning and content into the word "holy". For him God was not just *taboo.* He had actually shown Israel his holy nature through his righteous actions (Isa. 5:16). And since, for Isaiah, righteousness meant, not goodness, but compassionate care and creative love, that great prophet did more than anyone else to tell us the meaning of holiness. He even called God *the Holy One of Israel.* That title for God is written as only one word in Hebrew. Because this was so, the ordinary sinful people of Israel, by means of the name, learned to think of God's holy love as all bound up with what God had done in calling Israel to be his "son" (Exod. 4:22). H.H. Stamm has written: "Holiness is the nucleus of God's personality." And now Israel was being called to be holy, even as God himself is holy, that is to say, loving, compassionate, totally concerned for the world of men.

But there is still more to be said. The great prophets interpreted holiness as the power of God breaking into our human life, certainly not as some*thing* quite impersonal. That would be what the anthropologists call *mana* (taking the word from the New Zealand Maori). So God's holiness was the power of his loving, righteous, saving *presence* in Israel's midst. After looking at the Burning Bush, Moses had heard the words "I *am* with you", or perhaps better, "I shall be with you" (as your creative, loving, purposeful sustainer and guide).

THE LAW IS GOD'S GRACIOUS GIFT

What follows, then, are laws that God expects Israel to keep, if she is to continue to be the *holy community*. Israel here is not called to *become* holy (particularly by *doing* things, as by keeping these laws). Israel is not a heathen people that must be made holy by a process she must go through. God had already *made* her holy, by *separating* her (the word used at Lev. 1:17 and at Exod. 26:33) from all the other peoples of the earth. In doing this God was merely carrying on what he began to do at creation. For, as Gen. 1:4 puts it, God *separated* between light and darkness when he *began to create* (as we should say, following the footnote in the RSV at Gen. 1:1). So now, at Lev. 20:26 we read "You shall be holy to me; for I the Lord am holy, and have *separated* you from the peoples, that you should be mine." The result was that Israel now belonged to God, and so, by keeping the Law, she was set free from all the subtle tensions that the human person can go through. God's gift to Israel of the Law was thus an act of sheer grace on God's part. Israel had not earned it, and never could.

There is no thought anywhere in Leviticus that Israel is "better" than other peoples, or kinder, or wiser, or more philosophical, or more religious, or more civilized, or more cultured. What we meet with is just sheer amazing grace. Deut. 4:32–40 deals with this great fact quite specifically. Israel is to hold fast to the laws in the Holiness Code, not in order to *become* holy (for God had already made her so as a gift), but in order to *remain* holy, and so live and move and have her being in that holiness of living that belongs to God alone.

THE LAW AND THE COVENANT

The *Torah,* the Law of Moses, is what God *began* to give,

through Moses, to Israel. *Torah* was not given to just any people, nor was it meant for all peoples. God gave the *Torah* to the Covenant people alone, that people with whom he had entered into a special relationship at Sinai (Exod. 19:5-6). Accordingly if any individual in Israel refused to obey God's laws, which were created to keep Israel a holy people, then that individual would have to suffer the terrible penalty of being "cut off" from the Covenant community; see e.g. Lev. 17:9. We shall note what this means as we read on. But if he should fall out, there were means whereby he could be brought back home into the fellowship of the holy congregation, means that could cleanse him of his sin of disobedience and rebellion (e.g. Lev. 16:29-30).

THE LAWS ARE FOREVER

These laws were meant to be perpetual—*for God had said so.* Yet in actual fact they have not turned out to be such. Neither Jews nor Christians keep them today exactly as we find them here. Even the modern Orthodox Jew does not now offer animal sacrifices at a Temple in Jerusalem. The Epistle to the Romans which Paul wrote for Gentile Christians made clear that in Christ the Christian was set free from every single one of the statutes found in the book of Leviticus. Then why do we bother to read it, and how could a statute given by God *for ever* come to be ignored, in varying degrees, by both Jews and by Christians today?

The answer to that question is to be found by placing Leviticus firmly into its setting in Torah. The first words of Genesis run: "When God began to create . . .". God has never stopped creating; in fact, the way he works is to keep on *re*-creating out of what he has already created, as well as out of sin, evil and chaos, and in so doing, renewing, transforming all things till that day when he will create a new heaven and a new earth (Isa. 66:22). God's Word, that is to say, his purpose and plan as spoken to Moses, and as acted out before the eyes of Pharaoh when he re-created Israel out of a rabble of slaves into a people for himself—that Word is alive, simply because God himself is the living God. Accordingly, when God gives Israel a statute that is to last for ever, he cannot change his mind and say: "I have decreed that this statute will no longer be valid after year so-and-so." No, the statute in question must stand.

On the other hand, it is true to the creative purpose of God that he has planned to re-create that same statute in a new and profound form, a form, however, that could not have come into being if it had not originally taken the form in which we find it in Leviticus. The whole book of Leviticus is an instance of this truth. The first sixteen chapters deal largely with the issue of the proper relationship that is to be maintained between Israel and *God*. That is to say, how Israel is to love God with all her heart, soul, mind and strength. The second section, this Holiness Code, deals largely with how a man is to remain in holy fellowship with his brother *man*; and so it exemplifies the second of Jesus' two Golden Rules, "Thou shalt love thy neighbour as thyself".

Leviticus tells us what God began to do and teach from the days of Moses onwards. In the same way we read in Acts 1:1, "In the first book [our biblical Gospel of Luke], O Theophilus, I have dealt with all that Jesus *began* to do and teach until the day when he was taken up." In our day, then, we discover that the Holy Spirit, as referred to in John 15:26, led the early Church to *recreate* the teaching of Jesus to meet with new realms of experience unknown even to such a man as Luke. For example, the Church had to learn to get past the low understanding of God's Word that we meet with in the case of Peter's handling of the meanness of Ananias and Sapphira in Acts 5. Now we live in a period when we must apply the Word of God to such completely new situations as those which involve modern medical ethics, the use of the hydrogen bomb, the exploration of space, and so on. But in doing so, we keep holding on to the promise of God to Moses in the words "I will be with you", and, as Jesus adds, "even to the close of the age" (Matt. 28:20).

TWO EMPHASES ABOUT SACRIFICE

Leviticus 17:1–16

And the Lord said to Moses, "Say to Aaron and his sons, and to all the people of Israel, This is the thing which the Lord has commanded. If any man of the house of Israel kills an ox or a lamb or a goat in the camp, or kills it outside the camp, and does not bring it to the door of the tent of meeting, to offer it as a gift to the Lord before the tabernacle of the Lord, bloodguilt shall be imputed to that man; he has shed blood; and that man shall be cut off from among his people. This is to the end that the people of Israel may bring their sacrifices which they slay in the open field, that they may bring them to the Lord, to the priest at the door of the tent of meeting, and slay them as sacrifices of peace offerings to the Lord; and the priest shall sprinkle the blood on the altar of the Lord at the door of the tent of meeting, and burn the fat for a pleasing odour to the Lord. So they shall no more slay their sacrifices for satyrs, after whom they play the harlot. This shall be a statute for ever to them throughout their generations.

"And you shall say to them, Any man of the house of Israel, or of the strangers that sojourn among them, who offers a burnt offering or sacrifice, and does not bring it to the door of the tent of meeting, to sacrifice it to the Lord; that man shall be cut off from his people.

"If any man of the house of Israel or of the strangers that sojourn among them eats any blood, I will set my face against that person who eats blood, and will cut him off from among his people. For the life of the flesh is in the blood; and I have given it for you upon the altar to make atonement for your souls; for it is the blood that makes atonement, by reason of the life. Therefore I have said to the people of Israel, No person among you shall eat blood, neither shall any stranger who sojourns among you eat blood. Any man also of the people of Israel, or of the strangers that sojourn among them, who takes in hunting any beast or bird that may be eaten shall pour out its blood and cover it with dust.

"For the life of every creature is the blood of it; therefore I have said to the people of Israel, You shall not eat the blood of any creature, for the life of every creature is its blood; whoever eats it shall be cut off. And every person that eats what dies of itself or what is torn by beasts, whether he is a native or a sojourner, shall wash his clothes, and bathe himself in water, and be unclean until the evening; then he shall be clean. But if he does not wash them or bathe his flesh, he shall bear his iniquity."

(1) *Sacrifices are to be made at one place only.* If a man offers a sacrifice out in the field—which is not "holy" ground—he must bring it into the sanctuary. For it is there that you find holiness. In this way the ordinary man is helped to discover that it is not *where* you sacrifice that matters, but *to whom,* for it is to the living God, not to the jinns of the desert. Today there are people who declare that they go to find God on a golf course. Others like to quote the poem: "One is nearer God's heart in a garden than anywhere else on earth." No, says the New Testament. God's own choice of "place" is the person of the Lord Jesus Christ.

(2) *God's gift of life.* The key phrase at verse 11 is "For the life of the flesh is in the blood". The God of the Old Testament is the "living" God. His basic gift to man, therefore, is the gift of life (Gen. 2:7). And so the Bible reveals a deep, basic reverence for life. Even an animal carcass is to be reverenced because it is a gift from God. Man may use it (a) for food, or (b) as a means for receiving forgiveness at the altar, that is to say, for regaining atonement, or at-one-ment, with the holy God. But man is to respect the blood that is in the animal's carcass, for it is the very vehicle of the life that has to be poured out. "It is the blood that makes atonement." So we can see how the New Testament writers turned to Leviticus to help them put into words the virtually indescribable depths of meaning we are presented with in the death of Christ.

DON'T DO WHAT THE PAGANS DO

Leviticus 18:1–21

And the Lord said to Moses, "Say to the people of Israel, I am the Lord your God. You shall not do as they do in the land of Egypt, where you dwelt, and you shall not do as they do in the land of Canaan, to which I am bringing you. You shall not walk in their statutes. You shall do my ordinances and keep my statutes and walk in them. I am the Lord your God. You shall therefore keep my statutes and my ordinances, by doing which a man shall live: I am the Lord."

"None of you shall approach any one near of kin to him to uncover nakedness. I am the Lord. You shall not uncover the nakedness of your father, which is the nakedness of your mother; she is your mother, you shall not uncover her nakedness. You shall not uncover the nakedness of your father's wife; it is your father's nakedness. You shall not uncover the nakedness of your sister, the daughter of your father or the daughter of your mother, whether born at home or born abroad. You shall not uncover the nakedness of your son's daughter or of your daughter's daughter, for their nakedness is your own nakedness. You shall not uncover the nakedness of your father's wife's daughter, begotten by your father, since she is your sister. You shall not uncover the nakedness of your father's sister; she is your father's near kinswoman. You shall not uncover the nakedness of your mother's sister, for she is your mother's near kinswoman. You shall not uncover the nakedness of your father's brother, that is, you shall not approach his wife; she is your aunt. You shall not uncover the nakedness of your daughter-in-law; she is your son's wife, you shall not uncover her nakedness. You shall not uncover the nakedness of your brother's wife; she is your brother's nakedness. You shall not uncover the nakedness of a woman and of her daughter, and you shall not take her son's daughter or her daughter's daughter to uncover her nakedness; they are your near kinswomen; it is wickedness. And you shall not take a woman as a rival wife to her sister, uncovering her nakedness while her sister is yet alive.

"You shall not approach a woman to uncover her nakedness while she is in her menstrual uncleanness. And you shall not lie carnally with your neighbour's wife, and defile yourself with her. You shall not give any of your children to devote them by fire to Molech, and so profane the name of your God: I am the Lord."

Egypt was a pagan nation. In Moses' day the people worshipped some eighty different gods. Some of these were the manifestations of human violence, nationalistic chauvinism, or lust for power; others again were the apotheosis of mere sexual lust. This, too, is how the ancient Greeks thought of their gods.

There are some schools of sociologists and anthropologists who declare that man has always created his gods in the likeness of himself, by just throwing his own image up into the sky, so to speak. As a result of listening to such teaching at school, many a questing young person today turns away from all religion in disgust. The Old Testament, on the other hand, is the complete exception to this theory. It declares that the living God made man in *his* image (Gen. 1:26) and not the other way round. The result is as Leviticus insists, that if a man remains in fellowship with the living God then he really *lives*. This word does not describe the mere business of breathing that is common to all men. It speaks of that fulness of life which comes only from the God who is fully alive himself, and who is not an image of little man.

We have seen that chapters 1–16 have dealt primarily with man's relationship to God, how, in fact, man is meant to love God. Now at verse 6 we begin to learn how man is meant to love his neighbour as himself. In fact this chapter reads like a ready-made sermon for priests to use some Sabbath day!

Beginning at home, a man is to reverence the members of his own family. They are not to be the objects of his egotistical lust and violence, as Israel had seen take place in Egypt. While the list seems to cover all the possible relationships within the extended family group, we are to remember that the whole congregation of Israel is regarded as the family of God, and so as the Holy Family. 2 Sam. 13:12 shows how this particular *Torah* had been assimilated even as early as the beginning of the period of the monarchy. Amnon lusted after his half-sister, Tamar. "Come, lie with me, my sister", he begged. "No, my brother", she answered him, "do not force me, for such a thing is not done in Israel." We see there how the basic meaning of the word "holy" was taking root in the minds of ordinary people. We see in this story how to violate Tamar's holiness was a sin against both God and man. Note that the words "unclean" and "defile" both have to do with "making unholy".

Below the south-west wall of Jerusalem, there was a gorge

known as the Valley of Topheth, or Hinnom (this latter was a man's name; probably he was the original owner of the property) where the city's garbage and rubbish were dumped, and then burned. This fire never seemed to go out, for it was used so much. The Hebrew for "valley" is *ge*. By New Testament times the place of this "everlasting" fire had become known as *gehenna*, the second word being the Greek spelling of the name of the man Hinnom. This place of burning actually lay up against the wall of the *Holy City!* It did not lie away far off where Azazel dwelt. So it became the symbol of the everlasting judgment of God. Note that this judgment was directed, not against the Egyptians, or later on when we reach New Testament times, against the Romans, but against the Holy City itself. Isaiah makes full use of this potent imagery at Isa. 9:18–19 and 10:16–17. So it may come as rather a shock to us to learn that, in the Bible, while of course all men are under judgment, for all men are sinners, God's fires of judgement (hell-fire, if you like), are directed not at the heathen nations of the world, but at his own holy people (Amos 3:1–2).

One of the abominable cults of the Canaanites was the worship of their god Molech (which just means "king") by ceremonially throwing babies into this fire—to the glory of their god! (See Deut. 18:10.) Whether the babies were new-born, male or female, or even aborted foetuses, we do not know. The last is likely, since this one single verse (21) is sandwiched between two other verses that deal with sex. But the God of Israel who gives man life is profaned by murder in any form. The horrible practice was evidently copied by some Israelites from time to time, as we learn from 2 Kings 17:17; 23:10, and from Jer. 32:35.

HOMOSEXUALITY

Leviticus 18:22–30

"You shall not lie with a male as with a woman; it is an abomination. And you shall not lie with any beast and defile yourself with it, neither shall any woman give herself to a beast to lie with it: it is perversion.

"Do not defile yourselves by any of these things, for by all these the nations I am casting out before you defiled themselves; and the land became defiled, so that I punished its iniquity, and the land vomited out its inhabitants. But you shall keep by statutes and my ordinances and do none of these abominations, either the native or the stranger who sojourns among you (for all of these abominations the men of the land did, who were before you, so that the land became defiled); lest the land vomit you out, when you defile it, as it vomited out the nation that was before you. For whoever shall do any of these abominations, the persons that do them shall be cut off from among their people. So keep my charge never to practise any of these abominable customs which were practised before you, and never to defile yourselves by them: I am the Lord your God."

Two other abominable customs are mentioned, both of which were evidently practised by the indigenous Canaanite population. One was that of homosexual activities, and the other was human copulation with animals. The penalty for such practices was excommunication from the fellowship of the holy people of the holy God.

Since the question of homosexuality is a vexed one today throughout the whole Christian world, it is worth taking note of the manner in which Jesus interpreted the Law of Moses for his day and for his disciples. So what follows is by way of being an "excursus" on how we are to interpret and use the Law of Moses today.

Jesus looked back at the Old Testament realistically. He did not see it as being on one flat level of revelation. Never for him the modern idea that you can take a pin and stick it in at whatever verse you chance to open the Bible, and declare that the words you then read are the voice of God to you just as they stand. They may of course speak to you loudly at that moment in your life, but that is another issue. The fact that people used to take individual verses out of relation to their context is excusable, since they lived before the period when men came to see that we are to look at the Bible *historically;* for of course it is both a historical document and Holy Scripture at the same time. For example, people used to take the verse "Thou shalt not suffer a witch to live" (Exod. 22:18, "sorceress" in the RSV) as on a par with a verse that Jesus quotes from Gen. 2:24, "Therefore a man leaves his father and his mother and cleaves to his wife, and they become one flesh", merely because they both occur in the Bible. The result was the tragedy we all know about, how eccentric old ladies who perhaps had garbled stories to tell about how they had met Auld Nick at the bottom of the garden, or imagined that they could foretell a person's future by studying their palm, were burned at the stake or drowned in the village pond. This happened to old women only, let us note, because this verse in Exodus mentions only females! We know, however, that there are as many simple old men as there are simple old women.

However, Jesus did not approach the Old Testament in this way, and we would do well to learn from him. Moreover, we are now able to substantiate what he believed about the first eleven chapters of Genesis, that they were not written as "history". We know today that the material in those chapters is very ancient. Their contents were evidently handed down by word of mouth in the days when only very few could read and write, and when there was, in any case, little writing material to write on! But then, probably during the reign of Solomon, about 950 B.C., someone transcribed the ancient material (basically what we have in Genesis 2–11) in written form. Moreover, he did so in a manner that showed tremendous genius, or, as we might like to add, and as Jesus clearly believed, under the inspiration of the Holy Spirit. He did not write history, he wrote theology. In order to make his theology intelligible to educated and uneducated alike, to people of all cultures and of all periods of man (and today we think of such diverse types as the Chinese, the Bushmen of Africa and the Aborigines of Australia), he wrote that theology in a series of pictures. Jesus copied from Genesis this way of expressing truth, of telling forth the Word of God, when in his turn he used pictures to express his message. The result is that people of all cultures and all ages can grasp what he had to say with ease, because he spoke in parables—while unlettered persons find it hard to follow Paul's compact reasoning.

But the Law of Moses is different. Jesus believed that God had given the Law to Moses to fit that stage in the education of the people of Israel in which they required clear guidelines. Even today children need and appreciate rules and regulations; but when they grow into adulthood, then, as Paul puts it, they should have given up drinking their mother's milk and taken to eating strong meat. That is why Jesus can say of the Law of Moses, even of the Ten Commandments (see Matt. 5:27; Mark 2:27), that these applied only temporarily, that is to say, only for the period when God's "son" Israel was growing up. Consequently Jesus had to add the words: "But I say unto you ...".

AN EYE FOR AN EYE

Leviticus 18:22–30 (*cont'd*)

We can take the case of "An eye for an eye and a tooth for a tooth" as an example of the way Jesus looked upon the Law of Moses. There are those who, rejecting the Christian faith, scoff at this "law" in that it is to be found in the Bible. They ridicule the idea that the Christian could accept such a dictum as coming from a God of love. But if they were at all scholarly, and would only be willing to look at the Bible *historically,* our objectors would have to admit the tremendous advance in social ethics which this verse represents in light of what both ancient (and modern!) man is really like.

Jesus handles this verse, not by saying, "You've got to believe it and obey it because it is in the Bible", but by referring his hearers back to Genesis, to the *relevation* there of God's mind about what man is really like. Clearly Jesus regarded Genesis 1–11 quite simply as such revelation. In Genesis 4 we read how Cain murders his brother Abel. Cain is a typical case of the ordinary man, since he is the son of Adam and Eve, in other words, of humanity as we know it composed both of male and female. But mankind (male or female) has a genius for making things more evil than they actually are (see Gen. 6:5, and Mark 7:20–23, where Jesus says the same thing in words that meant something in A.D. 30). Cain has a descendant (evil has "snowballed" by the time he arrives on the scene) named Lamech (Gen. 4:23–24). Lamech has two wives, despite the absolute "word" of God in Gen. 3:24, so he has rejected his chance of being able to know or understand the meaning of love, compassion and total commitment. He shouts to them: "I have murdered a man just because he punched me on the jaw" (as we could say). "If Cain is avenged sevenfold, truly Lamech seventy-sevenfold."

The Law of Moses did a remarkable service to humanity at this point. We can observe vengeful groups or individuals to this day who behave just as Lamech boasted. We can think of the Mafia in the States, of hereditary vengeance going on for generations between tribes and families in the Near East, each killing calling for an answering killing, indefinitely and unendingly. We can recall cases where, in partisan warfare as in Yugoslavia during World War II, one side would declare, "If you slay one of the hostages or prisoners you have taken, we shall retaliate by slaying ten of yours." But Moses' Law said "No" to all that. One for one, one eye for one eye, one tooth for one tooth, one life for one life.

Now we turn to what Jesus has to say in the matter. Recognizing that the Law of Moses is of a temporary nature, Jesus first points this out. With respect to the second half of the Golden Rule which appears in Leviticus 19:18, Jesus says: "You have heard that it was said, 'You shall love your neighbour and hate your enemy'. But I say to you, Love your enemies...". Hating your enemy who is your neighbour is shown when you do not love him. Legislation for such non-loving, judgmental pronouncements can be seen at Exod. 21:15; 22:18 and elsewhere, and again at the point we have reached in Leviticus 18:22–30. Vengeance can only too easily be cloaked by what man self-righteously considers to be justice.

Jesus, however, makes a new approach. He goes behind the Law of Moses to the absolute statements in the Prologue to the Bible (Gen. 1–11). There we read that "The Lord saw that the wickedness of man was great in the earth, and that every imagination of the thoughts of his heart was only evil continually" (Gen. 6:5). We read in the Prologue that man's disobedience cut him off from "life in the Garden", and that God had to send him forth through the gate marked "Exit" into the land where there is no law and order. Then God had to place cherubim outside the "Way In" notice, with a flaming sword which turned every way, to "guard the way to the tree of life" (picture theology indeed!). Since man of his own free will has cut himself off from fellowship with God, as we see happens with Cain, keeping the Law will not bring him home to God again. For the Law can only regulate the kind of life that men must now live outside the Garden.

So far as that goes then, the Law is of course a gracious gift from God. But what man outside the Garden needs is not Law but a Saviour, one who can take him by the hand and walk him back from outside where he now is, past the flaming sword, into the peace and beauty of life with God in the Garden. Man cannot pull himself up by his own bootstraps. Man cannot build the perfect society by planning it out of his own head. Every human empire so far has eventually crumbled in the dust. Man cannot save himself. God put man out of the Garden, and so only God can bring him back in again. Isa. 43:11 declares this emphatically: "I, I am the Lord, and besides me there is no saviour." Even the name "Jesus" means "The Lord is Saviour". There cannot be two saviours. That is why Paul writes, "God was *in* Christ, reconciling the world to himself" (2 Cor. 5:19), or "bringing *the world* [not just individuals!] back into the Garden where God himself walks in the cool of the day, seeking the fellowship of the mankind whom he has created for himself" (Gen. 3:8).

JESUS AND THE LAW

Leviticus 18:22–30 *(cont'd)*

Lamech represents this reality about human nature and what man's life is like outside the Garden. Lamech lusts to take vengeance seventy-sevenfold. "One for one" may thus have been all right for the year 1000 B.C., and indeed that "law" was a remarkable bridle on human lust for dominance, violence, hatred and revenge. But Jesus was proclaiming a new era, one that was dawning with himself. It is because of this that he declares, "You have heard that it was said, 'An eye for an eye, and a tooth for a tooth'. But I say to you, Do not resist one who is evil. But if anyone strikes you on the right cheek, turn to him the other also" (Matt. 5:38–39). Only he who has such a love in his heart for objectionable people can even hope to begin the journey back into the Garden of God.

This whole new understanding of God's requirement of us in the face of violence, Jesus interpreted to Peter by referring him back to Lamech's boast—seventy-seven times. Moses had put the issue at one to one. Peter supposed that he had made a great advance upon Moses in suggesting that he forgive an insult seven times (Matt. 18:21–22). To which self-congratulatory statement (in that Peter was pleased with himself in showing so much self-control and strength of will to forgive) Jesus replied, "No, seventy-seven times" (see RSV footnote). What Jesus did was to turn over the coin marked "77" to let us see the back of it. Instead of destroying seventy-seven times, Jesus said "Recreate seventy-seven times", for forgiveness creates the life of the one whom you forgive. He gets a new chance, new hope, and new strength to go on. In other words, seventy-seven times, or seventy times seven (A.V.), whichever you like, describes the actions of one who has been turned right round. To forgive seven times, as Peter suggested was enough, was to show how self-controlled and high-minded Peter believed himself to be. But in forgiving an enemy indefinitely (as expressed by the number seventy-seven) reveals the nature of one who now has a new nature himself, one who can no longer even admit to himself that he has been insulted. Rather he now looks upon the man who has sinned against him with only mercy, compassion and love.

In the light of this long "excursus" therefore we now return to the verses before us to see what approach the Christian today should take to the question of homosexuality. Being now "a new man in Christ" he does not concern himself with the "question", the "issue" of homosexuality. He leaves the "question" of whether it is a disease that one can acquire, or inherit, or anything else, to the medical profession, or of whether homosexual behaviour is legal or not to the lawyer. This is because the Christian is now able to see the homosexual in an entirely new light. He sees him, not as Moses did, but as a *person,* a human soul whom God loves. Consequently, the Christian can approach the individual homosexual in only one way, and that one way echoes the love of Christ himself. For now he knows only one law, the law of love, and so of mercy, forgiveness, and that creative love which Christ has shown towards him.

Perhaps this discussion of how the modern Christian is to deal with such a command as we find at Lev. 18:22 will be a guide to how we are to approach all the other commands in this chapter, especially those dealing with sexual perversions. These all reflect the unexamined ways of people who worship gods who are themselves sexual perverts (vv. 24–25). But Israel now knows what the Holy One of Israel asks of his people if they are to be "holy, even as I am holy". "I am the Lord."

A SUMMARY OF THE LAW

Leviticus 19:1–4

And the Lord said to Moses, "Say to all the congregation of the people of Israel, You shall be holy; for I the Lord your God am holy. Every one of you shall revere his mother and his father, and you shall keep my sabbaths: I am the Lord your God. Do not turn to idols to make for yourselves molten gods: I am the Lord your God."

Chapter 19 offers Israel a useful and easily-learned summary of God's loving guidance for his people, meant, as they are, to live together as a happy family. This chapter, then, is a kind of guide-book for the families in Israel to use in their home life, rather than when they attend public worship.

God had brought Israel up out of Egypt. But God had not only rescued Israel *out of* Egypt, the Lord had led her *into* "a land flowing with milk and honey", one that was in great contrast to the wilderness conditions of Sinai. This land was the hill-country of Palestine which a small number of semi-civilized Semitic clans, going under various names, had occupied to varying degrees. So there was room in those hills for thousands more incomers to settle, just as, after the early Dutch settlers in South Africa had occupied as much of that empty land as they needed, there was still room for ever so many Bantu tribes to come south and settle also. The name Canaanite is the general name that Israel used for all those peoples who were already there when she arrived, such as the Amorites, Perizzites, Hivites, Jebusites and others. Now, the way of life of most of those various Canaanites tribes was nasty, brutish and often brutal.

We know from their literature, some of which has been discovered and deciphered in recent years, just how they lived their lives. This is because in their epic poems they tell us how their gods and goddesses behaved, and those divinities were created in the image of Canaanite man! These people, we have discovered, thought nothing of copulating with animals; we see that the males treated their women folk as mere objects of their lust; we have discovered that some of them burned their unwanted babies alive, under the guise of being religious. They were often mean and treacherous in both war and so-called peace; and they normally treated their slaves even as they treated their animals. Some of the "legislation" in Leviticus, therefore, is set down to warn Israel against Canaanite practices such as these.

It is in contrast to this degrading form of human existence that we are to see the miracle of this chapter. We can read through it verse by verse with the "Canaanite" way of life acting as a foil to what is written here, and so see it really as a "revealed" way of life. Moreover we are to remember as we read that we are dealing with a period a thousand years before Queen Boadicea lived and fought, at a time when our ancestors in Britain must have been merely painted savages with a way of life probably not much different from that of the contemporary Canaanites.

The rather simplistic phrase "The Lord said to Moses" represents the pictorial way the Old Testament uses to speak of "revelation". It means all that follows comes from God, was put into the heart of man by God; so the succeeding verses are not to be regarded as a mere summary of man's good ideas for the perfect society on earth, such as we find in the works of Plato and Aristotle. We are not going to receive either a sociological study or an economic blueprint for Israel's life in Canaan. We are to discover an outline for a totally new way of life in contrast to the life of the ancient civilizations of man.

So we note two things:

(1) This outline before us does not deal with "religion". Religion is what human beings think about God or the gods. Religion is a man-made activity. In fact, the word "religion" does not occur in the Old Testament. The Canaanite poems are well edited for us by the General Editor of this series, Dr. J.C.L. Gibson, in his *Canaanite Myths and Legends*. The Zen Buddhism that has reached us from Japan, or Moon's Unification Church that has come from Korea, are modern examples of varieties of "religion". But this chapter deals with ordinary life, with the institution of the family, with agricultural practice, with social behaviour, with the question of paying wages, with ensuring that correct weights and measures be used in the town's market place, and so on. In each case each activity has to be an expression of love.

(2) Man is to love his neighbour, simply because God himself *is* love. We read in Gen. 1:26: "God made man in *his*

image." Leviticus takes this sentence seriously and so describes the behaviour that Israel is meant to adopt.

YOU SHALL BE HOLY

Leviticus 19:1-4 *(cont'd)*

Israel is not a mere warring clan (nor must let itself become one!), but a *congregation*. The original meaning of the word in Hebrew is "a witnessing community". Surely that is a very theological statement. It is indeed, for it makes use of the influence of the great prophets of later centuries, whom it would be better to call theologians than prophets.

Thus, in contrast to the chaos in human relationships that marked the life of the Canaanites, family life was required to be holy. Such life was a *witness* to unbelievers. In Jesus' day, centuries after these words were penned, good Israelites heard a Gentile youth described as "a man without a father". For outside of Israel, family loyalty and love were so exceptional that many a child did not know who his father was. We can see why the New Testament revelation takes up at its very beginning with the story of the Holy Family. Moreover, today, when many young people see no difference between a church wedding and a civil wedding (at which no promises are taken in terms of loyalty, nor is the word "covenant" used as in the Old Testament), the emphasis of Leviticus on the holiness of family life is as relevant and as needed as it was in the days of the old Roman Empire into which Jesus was born. To this day in Israel, the mother (who is mentioned *first* here) is regarded as queen of the home. Moreover, the words "You must have consideration to the glory of your parents", as an old Jewish translation puts it, remind us of the words of Jesus about his Father, God, at John 7:18 and 17:1.

The question of keeping *my Sabbaths* is not regarded very congenially by many church folk today. We have at long last, they reason, emerged from a period (call it the Victorian era if you like) when the keeping of Sunday was a slavish exercise. Consequently, they feel, we don't want to return to such a legalistic view of that day which used to be called the Sabbath. But before agreeing with the modern mood we should note two contrasting realities about that special day.

(1) It is *my* Sabbaths of which we read. While the word Sabbath merely means "stop", and the idea of stopping work for a holiday goes far back into Near Eastern history, Israel believed that the regular every-seventh-day Sabbath was no mere human invention, but was a gift to Israel from God himself. Since it had come from God, it meant more than just "stop".

The point is that the institution of the Sabbath was God's chosen means of turning chaos into peace and joy. For example, the Canaanites expected their slaves to work all day and every day throughout an exhausting eighty-hour week. Of course they might give their slaves an occasional day off in order to celebrate a religious festival. But the Israelite Sabbath was different.

It was a "gift" to the *whole* "congregation", father, mother, child, boss, worker and slave, farmer, farm-labourer and entrepreneur alike. It was the gift of one whole day a week when *all* men could "stop", and not just the boss, to really rest their weary bones. It was a day when no one at all, absolutely *no one* dare shout at a farm-worker such words as, "Get on with your work, or else . . .". The Sabbath was therefore the symbol of the underlying unity of all men in the sight of God; it was the guarantee of the emancipation of the human spirit—man, it seemed, was not a mere animated machine. Man was a child of God. For on this one day a week *every* man was free to think about the meaning of life and the purpose of human existence; and in Israel's case he could meditate on the wonderful mystery of the nature of God. For it was the Lord, Israel's God, who had released Israel from the chaotic kind of "non-life" they had known under the lash of the taskmaster in Egypt, and who had then, through Moses, given them the guidelines of a new fulness of life that was dependent upon the opportunity that the Sabbath gave to think about what life under a loving God must mean. No wonder then that the next sentence runs: "Don't turn therefore to man-made gods" (or to human ideologies, as we might say): "*I* am the Lord your God", not Chemosh, or Molech, or Astarte—or Karl Marx!

(2) On two occasions in history, idealistic secular humanists have rid their people of the seventh day Sabbath. At the French Revolution two hundred years ago, and again at the Russian Revolution sixty years ago a tenth-day holiday was instituted instead of the ancient seventh day. In each case they had to revert soon to the seven-day week; working people actually broke down under the strain. The profound error made in both instances was to regard human beings as "hands", who could be made to work longer and produce more "for the good of society as a whole". Leviticus however regards workers as men and women made in the image of God, who need not only physical rest but a "holy day", one on which they can come close to God in worship and so rediscover the reason for doing any work at all!

ON BEING KIND

Leviticus 19:5–14

"When you offer a sacrifice of peace offerings to the Lord, you shall offer it so that you may be accepted. It shall be eaten the same day you offer it, or on the morrow; and anything left over until the third day shall be burned with fire. If it is eaten at all on the third day, it is an abomination; it will not be accepted, and every one who eats it shall bear his iniquity, because he has profaned a holy thing of the Lord; and that person shall be cut off from his people.

"When you reap the harvest of your land, you shall not reap your field to its very border, neither shall you gather the gleanings after your harvest. And you shall not strip your vineyard bare, neither shall you gather the fallen grapes of your vineyard; you shall leave them for the poor and for the sojourner: I am the Lord your God.

"You shall not steal, nor deal falsely, nor lie to one another. And you shall not swear by my name falsely, and so profane the name of your God: I am the Lord.

"You shall not oppress your neighbour or rob him. The wages of a hired servant shall not remain with you all night until the morning. You shall not curse the deaf or put a stumbling block before the blind, but you shall fear your God: I am the Lord."

In previous chapters we met with a detailed description of the *peace offering*. Now we see why Israel ought to perform such a cultic act. Israel must surely want to "keep the peace" and so to hold on to the God of peace. For, we should remember, in Hebrew the word peace, *shalom,* is the opposite of the word "chaos", "without form and void", that we find at Gen. 1:2. Israel dare not revert to the chaotic life of her neighbours now that the Lord has acted in grace, rescued her, and has offered her a beautiful way of life. Those who despise such an act of thanksgiving and loyalty, who do not keep up their worship of God in a regular manner, deserve to be excommunicated. Clearly they wish to become mere Canaanites in spirit. They prefer darkness to light. Some Israelites too might offer sacrifice perfunctorily, with their tongue in their cheek. Isa. 1 has strong words to say about such hypocrites. Isaiah declares that God hates play-acting in such matters. If people are to make their peace with God, they are to do so "so that you may be accepted".

But positively, the "holy family" of Israel is to show forth God's holy, rescuing love, by showing love, in turn, to the weaker and poorer members of the community, as well as to any foreigners who happen to be staying in the Holy Land. Why should such people experience either fear or hunger at all? In God's acre? And so once again we have the concrete way of showing God's mind that the Old Testament (and Jesus) delights to use. Instead of saying in a general sort of way that one ought to care for foreigners living in one's country, we now get, in verses 9 and 10, two pictures, both of which any uneducated peasant in Israel could easily grasp, for the cases fitted into his way of life. Each was an instance of how you should actually *do* the loving thing, and not just talk about it. The passage doesn't mean that you are to do only those two thoughtful and kindly acts mentioned. It means that these two particular acts are typical of what you should be doing all the time in all aspects of life.

Thus these clauses in the Law of Moses are not limited to the life of peasants in the ancient world. The spirit behind them might be expressed equally well in instances drawn from the modern money-orientated capitalistic society in which we are living now. So we might set ourselves the question of how to transfer to modern life the meaning of the Hebrew at verse 10: "You are not to strip your harvest field bare in a bad temper".

Interspersed among these very practical commands we find references to the Ten Commandments. Thus we are reminded that we are to think constantly how these great basic statements from God are to work out in ordinary life. For they apply equally to the life known to King David and to the vastly different and highly complex life of our twentieth century.

The command, "Thou shalt not steal", means more than just robbing a neighbour. For example, being slack in handing a labourer his wages when he is hired by the day is actually a form of robbing him. For the poor man is utterly dependent upon the coin you have agreed to pay him (it was one *denarius,* the Roman coin, in Jesus' day—see Matt. 20:2); for without it his wife and family will have to go without their supper. Today we think of robbery as a crime against the law. Leviticus regards it rather as a crime against love.

How clear such an awareness is we see at verse 14. The poorest persons in any community are the blind and the deaf, for they cannot earn their bread at all. And in those days there was no Social Security to fall back on! To be mean and vicious towards such helpless members of the "holy community" is to open the window to let in some of the moral chaos that lies in the air outside and allow it to disrupt Israel's special kind of life. Thus the man who puts a stumbling block in front of a blind man and then robs him of his wallet is living out what chaos means in our human life.

JUSTICE

Leviticus 19:15-18

"You shall do no injustice in judgment; you shall not be partial to the poor or defer to the great, but in righteousness shall you judge your neighbour. You shall not go up and down as a slanderer among your people, and you shall not stand forth against the life of your neighbour: I am the Lord.

"You shall not hate your brother in your heart, but you shall reason with your neighbour, lest you bear sin because of him. You shall not take vengeance or bear any grudge against the sons of your own people, but you shall love your neighbour as yourself: I am the Lord."

Justice is to be the kind of justice that God himself dispenses. For God, the Old Testament reminds us, is the supreme Judge himself. It is easy to be partial to the case of the rich man, even though we know him to be in the wrong. But, just because you want to be kind, even as God is kind, you might possibly find yourself being partial to the poor man even though you see clearly that he is in the wrong. That won't do! To favour him just because he is weak is not impartial justice.

Again, telling tales against your neighbour is not mere lying. It is a form of injustice. This is because your neighbour doesn't know what you are saying about him. Slander like that can be a symptom of actual hatred. If your dislike of your neighbour is like that, then you may not have the "guts" to confront him with your allegations and give him the chance to refute them; for your emotion will render you biased in your own favour. That's not justice either. That is not how God thinks and acts with us.

So now we seem to hear quite naturally the phrase that follows: *You shall love your neighbour as yourself* (v. 18). Jesus picked it out of Leviticus from here, and then, in the spirit of the whole chapter, laid it alongside the command of God that he gave

Israel at Deut. 6:4: "And you shall love the Lord your God with all your heart, and with all your soul, and with all your might" (Mark 12:29–30). But to the last line Jesus added the words: "and with all your mind", that is to say, with your brain and intelligence as well.

This section now ends with God appending his signature, so to speak: "I am the Lord."

The whole book of Leviticus is in two parts. Chapters 1–16 explain how Israel is to keep the first half of the Golden Rule: "Thou shalt love the Lord thy God, with all thy heart . . .". The second part, beginning at chapter 17, makes crystal clear what it means to keep the second half of the Golden Rule, about loving one's neighbour. So it is at this point in reading Leviticus that we discover, as Jesus teaches us, how the particular divine commands are transmuted (or fulfilled) in him, certainly *not* abolished. And so they become capable of fitting into every form of society the world can show. The kind of hinge to understanding the connection between the two halves of the book is (looking a little ahead) at Lev. 19:22, for it joins the command to love our neighbour with the whole question of the forgiveness of sins.

What damage has been done, however, to the words of Jesus by those who do not know what the Hebrew of Leviticus means. The phrase, "You shall love your neighbour as yourself", does *not* mean that we are to love other people as much as we love ourselves. Quite the contrary. The Hebrew means: "Love your neighbour as a man like yourself." That is to say, your neighbour is a human being, and a sinner, just like you, who is longing to be noticed, to be valued, to be brought into fellowship, in fact, to be loved—all of which are things you would like to happen to you.

Can we possibly imagine Jesus loving himself in any way at all? The portrait that comes to life for us in the Gospels is of one who is completely and compassionately concerned for all the various kinds of people he meets on the road of life, so that, quite literally, he has no time left to "love himself". The very idea is, in fact, preposterous. Christ did the opposite—he "emptied himself". Of course we cannot exclude the idea that God wants us to feed and clothe ourselves and our family, and live at the level necessary to take our proper place in society, for it is there that we are meant to make our witness. Nor are we to neglect "a proper conceit" of ourselves, as children of the living God. Yet the emphasis is elsewhere. In Part 1 we saw what sin means to God, how he detests it, and yet how he is always waiting to receive the sinner back home into the fellowship of the people of God. So in Part 2 we ought to see that we are meant to behave likewise, to keep apart from sin, but to love the sinner back into the fold! Our Lord clarified this commandment powerfully at another point in his teaching, by telling his hearers to love their neighbour *as I have loved you.*

Now, curiously, just to show that God draws no dividing line between *cultic* requirements and the *moral law,* we suddenly revert (in verses 20ff.) to the question of adultery. Leviticus does so on the basis that for God's people holy living means doing what the holy God himself does. We recall that God's holiness was made known to Israel through his *creative love* and compassion. So Israel had now to show *creative love* towards the adulterer and the sexual pervert. The Bible possesses no sexual ethic. In the light of Lev. 19:17–18 it knows only *a love ethic.* Thus at this point we are led to ask the *next* question: "What does it mean for me to *love* the adulterer and the sexual pervert?" The judgment passed on the various forms of sexual perversion that are described in chapter 18 (and we might single out the case of the homosexual at 18:22 because of its topical interest today) is thus not God's last word upon the issue.

A theme that we meet with right through the whole Old Testament is that, beginning with the Exodus from Egypt, God liberates the oppressed, sides with the powerless, and suffers with the afflicted. Surely then we are now in the position to repeat with a new depth of meaning the second Golden Rule: "Love your homosexual neighbour, remembering that he is a man [a sinner] just like yourself."

A PRACTICAL HANDBOOK

Leviticus 19:19–37

"You shall keep my statutes. You shall not let your cattle breed with a different kind; you shall not sow your field with two kinds of seed; nor shall there come upon you a garment of cloth made of two kinds of stuff.

"If a man lies carnally with a woman who is a slave, betrothed to another man and not yet ransomed or given her freedom, an inquiry shall be held. They shall not be put to death, because she was not free; but he shall bring a guilt offering for himself to the Lord, to the door of the tent of meeting, a ram for a guilt offering. And the priest shall make atonement for him with the ram of the guilt offering before the Lord for his sin which he has committed; and the sin which he has committed shall be forgiven him.

"When you come into the land and plant all kinds of trees for food, then you shall count their fruit as forbidden; three years it shall be forbidden to you, it must not be eaten. And in the fourth year all their fruit shall be holy, an offering of praise to the Lord. But in the fifth year you may eat of their fruit, that they may yield more richly for you: I am the Lord your God.

"You shall not eat any flesh with the blood in it. You shall not practise augury or witchcraft. You shall not round off the hair on your temples or mar the edges of your beard. You shall not make any cuttings in your flesh on account of the dead or tattoo any marks upon you: I am the Lord.

"Do not profane your daughter by making her a harlot, lest the land fall into harlotry and the land become full of wickedness. You shall keep my sabbaths and reverence my sanctuary: I am the Lord.

"Do not turn to mediums or wizards; do not seek them out, to be defiled by them: I am the Lord your God.

"You shall rise up before the hoary head, and honour the face of an old man, and you shall fear your God: I am the Lord.

"When a stranger sojourns with you in your land, you shall not do him wrong. The stranger who sojourns with you shall be to you as the native among you, and you shall love him as yourself; for you were strangers in the land of Egypt: I am the Lord your God.

"You shall do no wrong in judgment, in measures of length or weight or quantity. You shall have just balances, just weights, a just ephah, and a just hin: I am the Lord your God, who brought you out of the land of Egypt. And you shall observe all my statutes and all my ordinances, and do them: I am the Lord."

How practical this "Handbook for Believing Families" is! In it God tells them:

(1) Not to let a cow breed with a horse. That would be unnatural.

(2) Not to sow cabbages on the same patch as barley. That would make their harvesting almost impossible.

(3) Not to wear a garment made by sewing several pieces of different material together. In wet weather the coat would come apart. The old Hebrews used the one coat by day, and covered themselves with it as a blanket at night. We remember that Jesus' tunic at the crucifixion was one made without a seam. So he did not break the Law even in this little regard (John 19:23). To God, the good life evidently includes practical issues such as these.

We continue (after the verses on adultery) with a practical lesson in fruit-growing. This is because husbandry is not a mere scientific exercise. The Hebrew of verse 23b says: "Then you shall recognize that its fruit needs to be circumcized". Apples and figs and dates are to remain *taboo* for three years after planting, and only then brought into the life of the people of God *by circumcision!* Today we would say rather, *by baptism.* A baby entered the community life by circumcision, and in this way became "holy". So Israel was to treat its fruit trees in the same way! Fruit trees are sacred things, for they feed man. So only then "shall their fruit be an offering of praise to the Lord", just as in the case of a baby.

Verse 26 refers once again to a practice of the Canaanites that was *not* to be copied. Those folk believed in magic, and used witchcraft to ward off evil influences. The verse might be paralleled with advice given to believers today not to bother with the columns in the daily papers written by astrologers. Evidently the practices mentioned here were just old taboos connected with their pagan rites.

But note verse 28, which our RSV translates wrongly by using the word "flesh". The Hebrew word covers the whole person, body, soul and spirit. The Old Testament folk were well aware that you cannot misuse your flesh without misusing your whole personality, your soul as well as your body.

Dabbling with the occult (v. 31) does in fact defile you, in that it interrupts your personal relationship with the holy God.

"Manners maketh man", man as he ought to be, man made in the image of God. You will naturally respect and honour your seniors (v. 32) if you are really in awe of the Senior of all.

The general command to love your neighbour is now spelled out in verses 33–37. New immigrants and new settlers (obviously no matter what their colour of skin—that question is *never* raised in the Old Testament) are not just to be accepted, tolerated, or even helped; they are to be *loved*! Shopkeepers are to be honest, for honesty is a way of loving. Imagine the revolution in modern business life if we were to apply this divine command in terms of our culture now. We remember how, when a young man came asking Jesus for guidance, "Jesus, looking at him, loved him". Can you see a prospective employer, the woman at the cash desk, the taxi driver, the slum landlord, looking at his customer, and *loving* him? Yet this is a divine *command,* one that God signs once again with the words "I am the Lord", meaning, "It is the Lord who is ordering you to do this". We know that this is meant because the word for "just" has two forms, masculine and feminine. The masculine form applies to God, the feminine to man. Here "just" is found in the masculine (v. 36). So a just balance is of the holy and loving God, not of the imperfect attempts of man at what *he* thinks justice means.

THE FAMILY COMES FIRST

Leviticus 20:1–9

The Lord said to Moses, "Say to the people of Israel, Any man of the people of Israel, or of the strangers that sojourn in Israel, who gives any of his children to Molech shall be put to death; the people of the land shall stone him with stones. I myself will set my face against that man, and will cut him off from among his people, because he has given one of his children to Molech, defiling my sanctuary and profaning my holy name. And if the people of the land do at all hide their eyes from that man, when he gives one of his children to Molech, and do not put him to death, then I will set my face against that man and against his family, and will cut them off from among their people, him and all who follow him in playing the harlot after Molech.

"If a person turns to mediums and wizards, playing the harlot after them, I will set my face against that person, and will cut him off from among his people. Consecrate yourselves therefore, and be holy; for I am the Lord your God. Keep my statutes, and do them; I am the Lord who sanctify you. For every one who curses his father or his mother shall be put to death; he has cursed his father or his mother, his blood is upon him."

This collection of material is harsher in its judgment upon the practice of incinerating babies than the short mention of it at 18:21. It is not the priests, but the people themselves, the Holy Nation, who are to stone the perpetrators of such an act. God has given man life, his basic gift. That gift is present in every embryo and every child. "Shall I give my first-born for my transgression, the fruit of my body for the sin of my soul?" asks Micah (Mic. 6:7).

This is one of the passages in the Old Testament that people today fasten on to, to declare that the God of the Old Testament is a fierce and cruel God. That, however, would be to judge the Old Testament from the point of view of modern social thinking. Israel did not react that way at all to such a command from God. The above is the general Semitic way of declaring that obedience to God is a life and death matter. One can stress that only in parabolic language. How else can one stress *for all time* that cheapening human life is a hellish thing to do, and that the whole nation should be shocked at the very notion? Note that even those who pretend not to know what is happening outside the walls of Jerusalem (out of sight, out of mind?) are to be "cut off" (more life and death language!), excommunicated, from amongst their own people equally with those who do in fact murder their children.

The phrase "playing the harlot after Molech" comes from the way in which some of the great prophets sought to describe the essence of Israel's faith. Hosea was the first to speak of Yahweh, "the Lord", as Israel's husband, and of Israel as Yahweh's bride. A century later Jeremiah did the same. It is to Hosea's words then that we must go back to learn the biblical meaning of marriage. God, the divine husband, is a jealous God, as any true husband ought to be. When he made covenant with Israel at Sinai he had promised to be faithful to his wayward bride—absolutely. Accordingly he expected his bride to be faithful to him—absolutely. If therefore Israel, whom God had called his "chosen" people, was attracted to the worship of any other god (or "husband"), she was thereby "going a-whoring after other gods". She was breaking up the monogamous relationship that ought to exist between her and her God. God is not of course jealous of other gods—how could he be when they didn't exist? He is jealous *for* Israel, that she should be faithful!

Leviticus, along with the rest of the Torah, applies all this to human marriage. The latter is a one-man, one-woman relationship that should remain "till death us do part". If one partner worships anyone or anything else, such as another woman, or golf, or self-interest, more than his divinely given partner, then he is "playing the harlot after Molech". It is the children who suffer most if the marriage is broken. So now we see why the Old Testament always links adultery with murder as the two greatest sins.

In verses 6ff. we are back again with the occult. Surely this is because this whole area of human curiosity separates a man from God. The witches' covens that one hears of from time to time in the papers betray the deep alienation of the human heart from the God of the Bible, who offers man his love and friendship.

Now verse 9 makes a very strong statement. Merely to curse

one's parents could bring the death penalty on a man. If we consider this to be an inexplicably severe judgment, we shall find the answer in the next paragraph. At the moment we are made aware that to separate oneself from the loving will and fellowship of the God who has chosen us is a deeply serious matter.

ADULTERY IS THE ROAD TO DEATH

Leviticus 20:10–27

"If a man commits adultery with the wife of his neighbour, both the adulterer and the adulteress shall be put to death. The man who lies with his father's wife has uncovered his father's nakedness; both of them shall be put to death, their blood is upon them. If a man lies with his daughter-in-law, both of them shall be put to death; they have committed incest, their blood is upon them. If a man lies with a male as with a woman, both of them have committed an abomination; they shall be put to death, their blood is upon them. If a man takes a wife and her mother also, it is wickedness; they shall be burned with fire, both he and they, that there may be no wickedness among you. If a man lies with a beast, he shall be put to death; and you shall kill the beast. If a woman approaches any beast and lies with it, you shall kill the woman and the beast; they shall be put to death, their blood is upon them.

"If a man takes his sister, a daughter of his father or a daughter of his mother, and sees her nakedness, and she sees his nakedness, it is a shameful thing, and they shall be cut off in the sight of the children of their people; he has uncovered his sister's nakedness, he shall bear his iniquity. If a man lies with a woman having her sickness, and uncovers her nakedness, he has made naked her fountain, and she has uncovered the fountain of her blood; both of them shall be cut off from among their people. You shall not uncover the nakedness of your mother's sister or of your father's sister, for that is to make naked one's near kin; they shall bear their iniquity. If a man lies with his uncle's wife, he has uncovered his uncle's nakedness; they shall bear their sin, they shall die childless. If a man takes his brother's wife, it is impurity; he has uncovered his brother's nakedness, they shall be childless.

"You shall therefore keep all my statutes and all my ordinances, and do them; that the land where I am bringing you to dwell may not vomit you out. And you shall not walk in the customs of the nation which I am casting out before you; for they did all these things, and therefore I abhorred them. But I have said to you, 'You shall inherit their land, and I will give it to you to possess, a land flowing with milk and honey.' I am the Lord your God, who have separated you from the peoples. You shall therefore make a distinction between the clean beast and the unclean, and between the unclean bird and the clean; you shall not make yourselves abominable by beast or by bird or by anything with which the ground teems, which I have set apart for you to hold unclean. You shall be holy to me; for I the Lord am holy, and have separated you from the peoples, that you should be mine.

"A man or a woman who is a medium or a wizard shall be put to death; they shall be stoned with stones, their blood shall be upon them."

The paragraphs beginning at verse 10 help us very pointedly to discover how the Bible is basically concerned with human life as it really is. These verses cover the same ground as some of chapter 18. But this time we discover that the sinner is not just to be excommunicated for his adultery, he is actually to die!

This strongly worded command is meant to reveal to us a very remarkable reality about God himself. We must now look at what it meant. The Law of Moses, we recall, with its many and various items, was given for Israel to accept and obey for the period before the coming of Christ, yet the grace and mercy of God always seems to keep shining through its various regulations in a manner that warms our hearts. By Jesus' day, for instance, there were two parties amongst the scholars of the Law who entered into controversy with him. There were (1) those who believed they must keep the Law literally. This group, by the way, evolved within the next century into Talmudic Judaism. But there were also (2) those who saw that in some respects the Law was meant to be understood rather more metaphorically. It is good to discover that Paul was educated in the latter school of thought.

This group kept in mind two aspects of their ancient Semitic heritage. (a) All the Semitic peoples (and the Hebrews were Semites) constantly sought to express their thoughts and even to utter their commands in the form of parables or picture language. Thus, for example, the Psalmist could say, and we have no difficulty in understanding what he meant, "The Lord is my rock, and my fortress . . . my shield, the horn of my salvation, my stronghold" (Ps. 18:2). (b) As Israel continued to worship the *living* God down the centuries, she had gradually learned to understand the meaning of the word "death", not just in biological terms, but to mean also the opposite of living.

Proverbs chapter 7 contains a fascinating poem. It too is virtually a parable. It speaks of an innocent but simple young man (one of God's "little children") falling into the trap set for him by an over-sexed married woman, whose husband is away from home on business. The young man becomes infatuated with this woman's charms. "All at once he follows her, as an ox goes to the slaughter; he does not know that it will cost him his *life.*" The poem ends with these words: "Her house is the way to Sheol, going down to the chambers of death." In this story, however, nobody executes this silly young man. What happens to him, rather, is that he finds he has lost any understanding of what real life is. For real life is based on true love, on total loyalty and complete commitment in partnership to one's spouse. Thus the opposite of such real life can be described only in terms of the death of the human spirit.

It is tragic that, in this permissive age in which we live, promiscuity is not regarded as a sin against God. The result is that modern man is now bearing the penalty of his egotism. He is discovering what it means to miss out on those true dimensions of love which give meaning to life; for without real love our days are a mere downhill tread to the gates of Sheol.

THE GRACE OF GOD

We come back in verses 22ff. to the basic fact in our life. It is that, in grace, God has chosen to act on our behalf before we can act for ourselves. Here he has given his people a unique chance to know the meaning of life. God had separated Israel off from all other peoples to be holy, "clean", and had given her as her possession a land flowing with milk and honey. Such an act on God's part deserves no other name than that of grace. Israel did not deserve such kindness.

So it is, in the same way, the Christian can look back over his life and say: Before I could choose "death", God separated me at my baptism from all that is unclean and unholy, and invited me to live my life in fellowship with him. He did so by giving me a heritage in his people. When it happened he had said: "You shall be mine, and I will never let you go". That too is grace indeed. Consequently there is nothing else I can decently do but humbly and loyally obey the revealed will of God, his *Torah,* in all my relationships, both with God himself, and with my family and neighbours. For that is exactly what God has asked me to do.

THE ODOUR OF DEATH (Text)

Leviticus 21:1–22:9

And the Lord said to Moses, "Speak to the priests, the sons of Aaron, and say to them that none of them shall defile himself for the dead among his people, except for his nearest of kin, his mother, his father, his son, his daughter, his brother, or his virgin sister (who is near to him because she has had no husband; for her he may defile himself). He shall not defile himself as a husband among his people and so profane himself. They shall not make tonsures upon their heads, nor shave off the edges of their beards, nor make any cuttings in their flesh. They shall be holy to their God, and not profane the name of their God; for they offer the offerings by fire to the Lord, the bread of their God; therefore they shall be holy. They shall not marry a harlot or a woman who has been defiled; neither shall they marry a woman divorced from her husband; for the priest is holy to his God. You shall consecrate him, for he offers the bread of your God; he shall be holy to you; for I the Lord, who sanctify you, am holy. And the daughter of any priest, if she profanes herself by playing the harlot, profanes her father; she shall be burned with fire.

"The priest who is chief among his brethren, upon whose head the anointing oil is poured, and who has been consecrated to wear the garments, shall not let the hair of his head hang loose, nor rend his clothes; he shall not go in to any dead body, nor defile himself, even for his father or for his mother; neither shall he go out of the sanctuary, nor profane the sanctuary of his God; for the consecration of the anointing oil of his God is upon him: I am the Lord. And he shall take a wife in her virginity. A widow, or one divorced, or a woman who has been defiled, or a harlot, these he shall not marry; but he shall take to wife a virgin of his own people, that he may not profane his children among his people; for I am the Lord who sanctify him."

And the Lord said to Moses, "Say to Aaron, None of your descendants throughout their generations who has a blemish may approach to offer the bread of his God. For no one who has a blemish shall draw near, a man blind or lame, or one who has a mutilated face or a limb too long, or a man who has an injured foot or an injured hand, or a hunchback, or a dwarf, or a man with a defect in his sight or an itching disease or scabs or crushed testicles; no man of the descendants of Aaron the priest who has a blemish shall come near to offer the Lord's offerings by fire; since he has a blemish, he shall not come near to offer the bread of his God. He may eat the bread of his God, both of the most holy and of the holy things, but he shall not come near the veil or approach the altar, because he has a blemish, that he may not profane any sanctuaries; for I am the Lord who sanctify them." So Moses spoke to Aaron and to his sons and to all the people of Israel.

And the Lord said to Moses, "Tell Aaron and his sons to keep away from the holy things of the people of Israel, which they dedicate to me, so that they may not profane my holy name; I am the Lord. Say to them, 'If any one of all your descendants throughout your generations approaches the holy things, which the people of Israel dedicate to the Lord, while he has an uncleanness, that person shall be cut off from my presence: I am the Lord. None of the line of Aaron who is a leper or suffers a discharge may eat of the holy things until he is clean. Whoever touches anything that is unclean through contact with the dead or a man who has had an emission of semen, and whoever touches a creeping thing by which he may be made unclean or a man from whom he may take uncleanness, whatever his uncleanness may be—the person who touches any such shall be unclean until the evening and shall not eat of the holy things unless he has bathed his body in water. When the sun is down he shall be clean; and afterward he may eat of the holy things, because such are his food. That which dies of itself or is torn by beasts he shall not eat, defiling himself by it: I am the Lord.' They shall therefore keep my charge, lest they bear sin for it and die thereby when they profane it: I am the Lord who sanctify them."

THE ODOUR OF DEATH (Commentary)

Leviticus 21:1–22:9

Now we can see the connection between physical death and the spiritual descent into Sheol. What we have here is echoed by Jesus when he declared "Let the dead bury their dead". His words are positive. They call for an attitude to *life*; they are not negative, as if to say, that man should *not* bury his dead. We remember how *Torah* proudly declares that God buried Moses on the top of Pisgah (Deut. 34:6), while Moses was still full of vitality and "life".

Physical death is an unholy thing. Jesus regarded it as the enemy along with sickness. Paul calls it the last enemy. Accordingly, even mourning signs used by pagans who think of it as the mere gateway to another world of the spirits of the dead should not be copied (v. 5). Moreover, all forms of defilement point to the reality of the power of this enemy. On the one hand, within the holy fellowship one finds holiness, purity, love and *life*. Excommunicated from it, on the other hand, there is only the odour of death. The priest, who administers the holy things, must of course be specially careful to set a good example in these matters.

This rule applies even more to the High Priest. He is the head of the body of Israel, so to speak, and must therefore make a clear witness. On the other hand, he is not a kind of arch-priest or arch-bishop. As the first amongst equals in the days of the great prophets, he was more like what we today call a moderator of a church court. His exaltation to a unique status actually took place only after the return from exile (Hag. 1:1). What is true for his public life must also be true for his home life. His marriage must show forth the beauty of holiness.

Just as the offering made to God on the altar was to be of an animal "without blemish" (3:6), so too with the offerer. The priest throughout all generations to come was to be free of every form of physical blemish. If he should be born deformed, or sustain an injury, then he could be precluded from becoming a priest; but such accidents did not prevent him from receiving "holy communion" (v. 22). What a powerful acted parable this description was of what a priest must be! Surely it helped Israel to reach the truth expressed by the Psalmist at Ps. 24:3–4:

> Who shall ascend the hill of the Lord?
>   And who shall stand in his holy place?
> He who has clean hands [physically] and a pure heart [spiritually],
>   Who does not lift up his soul to what is false,
> And does not swear deceitfully.

God is the all-holy One. Fools and the unclean dare not rush in where angels fear to tread.

In 22:1 ff. we are given further instances of the danger of uncleanness or "unholiness". For example, the ordinary man, if he has become unclean in any way, must get right with God before he dare bring forward his beast for sacrifice. So with the life of the Church today. In our worship patterns, the sinner must make confession and receive absolution before he can partake of holy communion. God's grace is not cheap grace, and God takes "unholiness" seriously.

We should not be surprised to learn that an emission of semen renders a man "unholy". Semen is God's vital gift to each male; without it he could not consummate a holy marriage. A holy marriage, we have seen, is an element in the total life of the holy people, in that the new couple together form a new family. But if this God-given creative fluid is not directed to its proper and holy use, then the holy thing itself becomes unholy. We recall how the manna in the desert was God's life-giving gift to Israel (Exod. 16). But when that same manna was misused, it stank. In parallel with this idea, verse 8 sensibly warns against eating meat that may have gone bad in the hot sun, or have come from an animal that has died of a disease.

Verse 9 brings to a head a very important Old Testament statement. It is that Old Testament man, unlike his pagan neighbours, and unlike modern secular man, was not afraid of death, evil thing that it was. How could he be afraid? Did he not belong in the Covenant people, the people to whom God had promised to be faithful *for ever?* What he did fear was separation from God, whether by sin or by disease (two aspects of the same thing, we recall). In this heritage therefore, Jesus, who also belonged in the Covenant, could say to the doubting Sadducees: "God is not the God of the dead, but of the living."

EMPHASIS ON THE FAMILY

Leviticus 22:10–33

"An outsider shall not eat of a holy thing. A sojourner of the priest's or a hired servant shall not eat of a holy thing; but if a priest buys a slave as his property for money, the slave may eat of it; and those that are born in his house may eat of his food. If a priest's daughter is married to an outsider she shall not eat of the offering of the holy things. But if a priest's daughter is a widow or divorced, and has no child, and returns to her father's house, as in her youth, she may eat of her father's food; yet no outsider shall eat of it. And if a man eats of a holy thing unwittingly, he shall add the fifth of its value to it, and give the holy thing to the priest. The priests shall not profane the holy things of the people of Israel, which they offer to the Lord, and so cause them to bear iniquity and guilt, by eating their holy things: for I am the Lord who sanctify them."

And the Lord said to Moses, "Say to Aaron and his sons and all the people of Israel, When any one of the house of Israel or of the sojourners in Israel presents his offering, whether in payment of a vow or as a freewill offering which is offered to the Lord as a burnt offering, to be accepted you shall offer a male without blemish, of the bulls or the sheep or the goats. You shall not offer anything that has a blemish, for it will not be acceptable for you. And when any one offers a sacrifice of peace offerings to the Lord, to fulfil a vow or as a freewill offering, from the herd or from the flock, to be accepted it must be perfect; there shall be no blemish in it. Animals blind or disabled or multilated or having a discharge or an itch or scabs, you shall not offer to the Lord or make of them an offering by fire upon the altar to the Lord. A bull or a lamb which has a part too long or too short you may present for a freewill offering; but for a votive offering it cannot be accepted. Any animal which has its testicles bruised or crushed or torn or cut, you shall not offer to the Lord or sacrifice within youı land; neither shall you offer as the bread of your God any such animals gotten from a foreigner. Since there is a blemish in them, because of their mutilation, they will not be accepted for you."

And the Lord said to Moses, "When a bull or sheep or goat is born, it shall remain seven days with its mother; and from the eighth day on it shall be acceptable as an offering by fire to the Lord. And whether the mother is a cow or a ewe, you shall not kill both her and her young in one day. And when you sacrifice a sacrifice of thanksgiving to the Lord, you shall sacrifice it so that you may be accepted. It shall be eaten on the same day, you shall leave none of it until morning: I am the Lord.

"So you shall keep my commandments and do them: I am the Lord. And you shall not profane my holy name, but I will be hallowed among the people of Israel; I am the Lord who sanctify you, who brought you out of the land of Egypt to be your God: I am the Lord."

The word "outsider" meant any unauthorized person who did not belong in the priest's extended family. But there were special cases made for other close relatives as well as what we would regard today as *au pair* girls. For all who worked within the home were part of the family unit. Just as it was the family that God had chosen as his "unit", so, in New Testament times, we see families being welcomed into the young Christian Church. Dare we say that, since the biblical knowledge of God is that he is Three in One, Trinity, he is in fact a family in his own divine being? It would be a good exercise, with the help of the concordance, to see how often the phrase "So-and-so, and his family", appears in the Old Testament.

There are those who see here a rather unfortunate idea. It is that "eating the holy thing" is meant for the elect alone. It seems that it is only the priest who really knows what he is doing when he handles the holy things. It seems that it would be dangerous to let the "layman" eat the holy thing on his own account. This view of a man's relationship to the "holy" was in part responsible for inducing the Church in medieval times to withhold the Bible from the people. True, an unlettered peasant in the old Holy Roman Empire might not have made much sense of the book of Leviticus without guidance! And he might possibly, in his boorish way, even spill the wine of the Sacrament down his beard. These are practical and natural fears that the Church entertained. But such is not the reason for this prohibition here. In fact, in this chapter, we are actually brought back to the purpose behind the whole biblical doctrine of election.

We read at Gen. 12:3 that God chose Abraham in order that Abraham's descendants might be a blessing to the world. We read at Exod. 19:5 that God chose Israel (1) to be a holy people, and (2) to be a kingdom of priests. A priest is one who serves, not himself, but his people. Then we read at Isa. 49:6 that Israel as a whole is elect, called, chosen (any of these words) to be "a light to the nations, that my salvation may reach to the end of the earth."

There are Christians today who suppose that they are chosen "to be saved"; so they think with horror of the millions who have never heard the name of Jesus, and who are therefore meant, even elected, to perish for ever. But this is a false understanding of election as we meet with it in both Testaments. Israel is elect, chosen, not to be saved, but to save and serve others. And so, if she rejects her calling to serve, and thus to be a blessing to the nations of the earth, it is she who will, in particular, be under judgment, and not just the great masses of "unredeemed" humanity. Jesus said: "You did not choose me; but I chose you and appointed you, *that you should go and bear fruit.*"

In the same way, then, since it was God who had elected the priest to *serve* Israel, he had to be forgiven like anyone else, and kept within the fellowship, and receive his daily bread. The priest was thus ministered to by God, that he might in turn minister to Israel. And the various feasts and sacrifices of which we have now learned, were there to uphold the Covenant that God had made with the *people* of Israel, who, through the Covenant, were to serve as a priest to the nations of the earth.

We note in verse 26 the interesting point, that just as a male child born within Israel had to be circumcized by his eighth day of life, thus ratifying his membership in the Holy Family, so here the animal to be sacrificed to keep him in the fellowship must be at least eight days old.

And just as a human mother and her son are two precious but separate personalities, so too in the case of the animals that are to be used for their maintenance in the holy community. In other words, this *Torah* (from the mouth of God!—see v. 26) emphasizes the value of animal life just as it values human life. We find the same thing expressed elsewhere in the Law. For example, the mother-bird is not to be taken along with her eggs (Deut. 22:6–7). This is a vivid way of saying that mere man must not exterminate a whole species of animal, bird or anything else, but must regard its life as sacred. Animals may be used for food, particularly the sacrificed animal, but the animal world must of necessity join in the basic creative act of sacrifice. God himself has willed it and also experiences it, even as he journeys *with* his people on their pilgrimage on earth. For the way of the Cross is God's chosen way to bring about the resurrection of all things. In line with the ancient poem in Deut. 32, God does not ask Israel to be vegetarian in diet, any more than he asks the animal world to be. To have done so would have side-stepped the whole significance of pain and suffering and so also of sacrifice and the Cross.

The chapter ends with the words: "You shall keep my commandments and do them." What we have looked at above is one instance of a commandment which Jesus "fulfilled", giving us thereby a whole new vista upon the immensity of God's love.

THE SACRED CALENDAR (Text)

Leviticus 23:1–44

The Lord said to Moses, "Say to the people of Israel, The appointed feasts of the Lord which you shall proclaim as holy convocations, my appointed feasts, are these. Six days shall work be done; but on the seventh day is a sabbath of solemn rest, a holy convocation; you shall do no work; it is a sabbath to the Lord in all your dwellings.

"These are the appointed feasts of the Lord, the holy convocations, which you shall proclaim at the time appointed for them. In the first month, on the fourteenth day of the month in the evening, is the Lord's passover. And on the fifteenth day of the same month is the feast of unleavened bread to the Lord; seven days you shall eat unleavened bread. On the first day you shall have a holy convocation; you shall do no laborious work. But you shall present an offering by fire to the Lord seven days; on the seventh day is a holy convocation; you shall do no laborious work."

And the Lord said to Moses, "Say to the people of Israel, When you come into the land which I give you and reap its harvest, you shall bring the sheaf of the first fruits of your harvest to the priest; and he shall wave the sheaf before the Lord, that you may find acceptance; on the morrow after the sabbath the priest shall wave it. And on the day when you wave the sheaf, you shall offer a male lamb a year old without blemish as a burnt offering to the Lord. And the cereal offering with it shall be two tenths of an ephah of fine flour mixed with oil, to be offered by fire to the Lord, a pleasing odour; and the drink offering with it shall be of wine, a fourth of a hin. And you shall eat neither bread nor grain parched or fresh until this same day, until you have brought the offering of your God: it is a statute for ever throughout your generations in all your dwellings.

"And you shall count from the morrow after the sabbath, from the day that you brought the sheaf of the wave offering; seven full weeks shall they be, counting fifty days to the morrow after the seventh sabbath; then you shall present a cereal offering of new grain to the Lord. You shall bring from your dwellings two loaves of bread to be waved, made of two tenths of an ephah; they shall be of fine flour, they shall be baked with leaven, as first fruits to the Lord. And you shall present with the bread seven lambs a year old without blemish, and one young bull, and two rams; they shall be a burnt offering to the Lord, with their cereal offering and their drink offerings, an offering by fire, a pleasing odour to the Lord. And you shall offer one male goat for a sin offering, and two male lambs a year old as a sacrifice of peace offerings. And the priest shall wave them with the bread of the first fruits as a wave offering before the Lord, with the two lambs; they shall be holy to the Lord for the priest. And you shall make proclamation on the same day; you shall hold a holy convocation; you shall do no laborious work: it is a statute for ever in all your dwellings throughout your generations.

"And when you reap the harvest of your land, you shall not reap your field to its very border, nor shall you gather the gleanings after your harvest; you shall leave them for the poor and for the stranger: I am the Lord your God."

And the Lord said to Moses, "Say to the people of Israel, In the seventh month, on the first day of the month, you shall observe a day of solemn rest, a memorial proclaimed with blast of trumpets, a holy convocation. You shall do no laborious work; and you shall present an offering by fire to the Lord."

And the Lord said to Moses, "On the tenth day of this seventh month is the day of atonement; it shall be for you a time of holy convocation, and you shall afflict yourselves and present an offering by fire to the Lord. And you shall do no work on this same day; for it is a day of atonement, to make atonement for you before the Lord your God. For whoever is not afflicted on this same day shall be cut off from his people. And whoever does any work on this same day, that person I will destroy from among his people. You shall do no work: it is a statute for ever throughout your generations in all your dwellings. It shall be to you a sabbath of solemn rest, and you shall afflict yourselves; on the ninth day of the month beginning at evening, from evening to evening shall you keep your sabbath."

And the Lord said to Moses, "Say to the people of Israel, On the fifteenth day of this seventh month and for seven days is the feast of booths to the Lord. On the first day shall be a holy convocation; you shall do no laborious work. Seven days you shall present offerings by fire to the Lord; on the eighth day you shall hold a holy convocation and present an offering by fire to the Lord; it is a solemn assembly; you shall do no laborious work.

"These are the appointed feasts of the Lord, which you shall proclaim as times of holy convocation, for presenting to the Lord offerings by fire, burnt offerings and cereal offerings, sacrifices and drink offerings, each on its proper day; besides the sabbaths of the

Lord, and besides your gifts, and besides all your votive offerings, and besides all your freewill offerings, which you give to the Lord.

"On the fifteenth day of the seventh month, when you have gathered in the produce of the land, you shall keep the feast of the Lord seven days; on the first day shall be a solemn rest, and on the eighth day shall be a solemn rest. And you shall take on the first day the fruit of goodly trees, branches of palm trees, and boughs of leafy trees, and willows of the brook; and you shall rejoice before the Lord your God seven days. You shall keep it as a feast to the Lord seven days in the year; it is a statute for ever throughout your generations; you shall keep it in the seventh month. You shall dwell in booths for seven days; all that are native in Israel shall dwell in booths, that your generations may know that I made the people of Israel dwell in booths when I brought them out of the land of Egypt: I am the Lord your God."

Thus Moses declared to the people of Israel the appointed feasts of the Lord.

THE SACRED CALENDAR (Commentary)

Leviticus 23:1–44 (*cont'd*)

We recall the line of the well-known hymn: "The sacred year has now revolved", the word "sacred" referring to festivals whose sources are to be found in the Bible. Thus it means Advent, Christmas, Lent, Easter and so on, and so does not refer to the calendar that runs from January 1st to December 31st. This chapter 23 gives us another sacred calendar, one that was to be kept by Israel, the people of God, in Old Testament times.

We note that this calendar was marked by "holy convocations", holy both because they had to do with the holy God, and because they were aids to keep Israel "holy, even as I am holy". That is why God calls them here *my* festivals.

First there is the weekly Sabbath. It is of course a holy *convocation,* that is, a time when people are called together, as the word means, to celebrate the goodness of God. No one keeps the Sabbath properly if he is all alone. You keep it with your children, with your neighbours and with your friends. We have already seen that the Sabbath is (1) a day of rest. Now we discover (2) that it is a day for common worship. We can see how the original early laws had to be modified to fit the period when Israel's population had grown and many people lived a long way from the Temple. The emphasis therefore is upon keeping the festivals at home with the family and in the village synagogue, even though the ritual at the Temple continues (as at v. 12).

Israel's "birthday" was the first Passover, of which we read at Exod. 12 and Deut. 16. It celebrated the day when God rescued his people from slavery in Egypt so as to make them his servants to do his will in the world. We pause to note that the various "liberation" movements of our time: Women's Liberation, Gay Liberation, liberation from colonialism, the activities of the various Red Brigades, and so on, are not acting in accordance with the mind of God if they seek *only* to obtain freedom. The Passover is a religious *act*. Since the Last Supper fell upon the night of the Passover, we are not surprised to read Paul's description of it too as an *act*. Then he goes on to say that Jesus has ordered us to *act* in accordance with his act; "This *do*", he said (1 Cor. 11:25). We have to *do* something after God has liberated us. We must take the second step of entering into willing service to God who seeks to use us for the world of men. Thus we give up the freedom we have just been granted in order to enter the service of God. If we do not do so, then our new-found freedom turns into licence. And since the Passover is repeated each year, it reminds us all that God did not save only once, but continues to be our Saviour and still remembers his Covenant (Isa. 43:11–12).

How attractively naive some verses of Leviticus are! At verse 11 we read that, once the Passover and the barley-harvest had been unified, the priest drew God's attention to the fact that Israel had done so by waving a sheaf of barley before the Lord The Passover went back only to the days of Moses. The "first-fruits" ceremony was much more ancient. Israel took it over from her neighbours and "baptized" it into her sacred year. The whole people of Israel were God's first-fruits amongst the nations. At Exod. 4:22 we read that Israel was God's "first-born son". The people of Israel thanked God for choosing them out of all the nations of the earth to serve him, and linked that with thanking him for feeding and clothing them with so many good things. The two are mentioned together at Mark 14:1–2. In Palestine the rains come in the period October-December each year. By our Christmas period, then, the grain is sown in the wet ground and harrowed in. Throughout February and March there are light, intermittent rains, ideal to help the grain to swell. *Barley* is usually the first to be ready. So it was harvested around our Easter time.

Fifty days later (*pentecost* is the Greek for fifty) came the *wheat* harvest, and so Israel celebrated the *Feast of Seven Weeks.* The early Church saw that date as representing the *Harvest of the Spirit,* when the spirit of peace (v. 19) was shed upon her. Understandably, the sacrifice offered on that day would bring peace, *shalom,* or reconciliation: at-one-ment between God and man (v. 19).

The editor of Leviticus includes a little note here at verse 22 that fits in with any or all of the commandments given in this chapter. "Once you were poor and hungry, and a stranger in a strange land. Now that I have set you free, you must remember you are free only to be my servants. I love the poor and the displaced persons, therefore you must be as kind to all strangers in your land as I have been to you", says God. This command is echoed and expanded by Jesus when he said in the most concise manner: "Love one another, *as I have loved you.*"

THE FEAST OF INGATHERING OR NEW YEAR

Leviticus 23:1–44 (*cont'd*)

We are now, at verse 23, into September. July and August were arid, rainless months. But the vineyards prospered, for the roots of the vine go deep and do not need surface rain. The grape-harvest came in September. Then followed a whole week of holy days, and this particular week the Jewish people observe to this day.

(1) First, there was an *extra Sabbath* rest, for the people would be very tired after the grape harvest.

(2) Then followed the *Day of Atonement,* as we saw in chapter 16. It too was a very special Sabbath.

(3) Then came the *Feast of Booths,* or *Tabernacles,* which lasted for a week. Families were enjoined to erect flimsy shelters made of the branches of trees, or by weaving together willow withes. They were to live out-of-doors in these shelters for the whole week. Doing this would remind them of their days in the Wilderness in the time of Moses. They were in fact, in the Promised Land, living in stone houses. But they were never to forget that the Covenant people dare not "dig in" in this life, or say that the things that money can buy are all that we need: "We don't have to think about God and his purposes any more!" Israel was reminded that they were still pilgrims on the march from birth to death. Now that they were living a settled life, they were to hold a thanksgiving service for the produce of the land. And they were to remember that they did not own the land or hold it for ever. Yet God is the God both of nature, in giving his people food out of the ground, and of history, in marching *with* them all the forty long years in the Wilderness. In these ways Israel learned to put together these two truths about God.

Then came a great climax to this week of events. On the last day, in later years, the High Priest marched down from the Temple to the Pool of Siloam with a great golden pitcher on his head. With appropriate prayers and actions, he scooped up water from the Pool, and carried it in triumph up the great staircase that had been built by Jesus' day and returned to the Temple. Thereupon, after a *spoken* prayer, he poured the water from the pitcher over the altar. By doing this he was *acting a prayer.* The point was that unless the rains began to come again, now that the harvest was in, the new cycle of the agricultural and pastoral year could not begin. So the High Priest prayed to God for rain to recommence. But by Jesus' day, along with that prayer, another had come into being. The gift of rain was regarded as the outward sign of the gift of the Holy Spirit. So the High Priest besought God to pour forth his spirit once more on Israel. It was at that dramatic moment that the excited crowd of worshippers heard Jesus cry out loud: " 'If anyone thirst, let him come to me and drink ... Now this he said about the Spirit ..." (John 7:37-39).

GOD IS LIGHT

Leviticus 24:1-9

The Lord said to Moses, "Command the people of Israel to bring you pure oil from beaten olives for the lamp, that a light may be kept burning continually. Outside the veil of the testimony, in the tent of meeting, Aaron shall keep it in order from evening to morning before the Lord continually; it shall be a statute for ever throughout your generations. He shall keep the lamps in order upon the lampstand of pure gold before the Lord continually.

"And you shall take fine flour, and bake twelve cakes of it; two tenths of an ephah shall be in each cake. And you shall set them in two rows, six in a row, upon the table of pure gold. And you shall put pure frankincense with each row, that it may go with the bread as a memorial portion to be offered by fire to the Lord. Every sabbath day Aaron shall set it in order before the Lord continually on behalf of the people of Israel as a covenant for ever. And it shall be for Aaron and his sons, and they shall eat it in a holy place, since it is for him a most holy portion out of the offerings by fire to the Lord, a perpetual due."

Symbolism is very important to faith. God is Spirit, man is merely creature. Consequently man cannot conceive what God is like in himself. Yet the whole *Torah* (Gen.–Deut.) believes that the living God is actually *present* with his people. So we put two things together. (1) God had said to Moses: "I will be *with* you" (Exod. 3:12). But since Moses was the "head" of the "body" of Israel, so God would be with all his people. (2) In the beginning of creation God had said: "Let there be light" (Gen. 1:3). And ever since then light had been a symbol of God's creative power and love. A Psalmist can say: "The Lord *is* my light and my salvation" (Ps. 27:1). The New Testament declares: "It is the God who said, 'Let light shine out of darkness', who has shone in our hearts to give the light of the knowledge of the glory of God in the face of Christ" (2 Cor. 4:6). So here "Aaron" (that is, the long succession of priests descended from Aaron) puts together these two truths about God: (1) God is *with* us, that is, he is Immanuel, and (2) God is light. The light is to burn continually in the Tent of Meeting, the holy place where God meets particularly *with* his people as saving love.

Israel must learn, through another symbolic act, to make her weekly offering to the Lord. We learn here that we do not "make a collection" in church; that would be merely a secular activity. Rather, we "take up an offering". This is because what we give goes to the Lord. David said to Araunah in his old age, "I will not offer burnt offerings to the Lord my God which cost me nothing" (2 Sam. 24:24). When he said that, little did he know that the land he was purchasing would one day become the site of Solomon's Temple.

The ingredients of the cakes mentioned here are to be only of the finest and best. We cannot know what God will do one day with our weekly offering *provided we give him the best we have*. It costs money to keep a church going. The priest or minister, like the labourer, is worthy of his hire (v. 9)!

But there is still another point to note here. The offering is not just to be *my* offering, any more than in the Lord's Prayer are we taught to say: "*My* father who art in heaven . . .". We are not just individuals. We are limbs in the body of the people of God. The people's offering is laid before God in twelve lots. This is because Israel is made up of twelve tribes. So in this way, Israel learns that it is her whole combined "self" that is laid on the altar, an altar of pure gold, such as might be worthy to receive her love and gratitude to God.

THE MEANING OF BLASPHEMY

Leviticus 24:10–23

Now an Israelite woman's son, whose father was an Egyptian, went out among the people of Israel; and the Israelite woman's son and a man of Israel quarrelled in the camp, and the Israelite woman's son blasphemed the Name, and cursed. And they brought him to Moses. His mother's name was Shelo'mith, the daughter of Dibri, of the tribe of Dan. And they put him in custody, till the will of the Lord should be declared to them.

And the Lord said to Moses, "Bring out of the camp him who cursed; and let all who heard him lay their hands upon his head, and let all the congregation stone him. And say to the people of Israel, Whoever curses his God shall bear his sin. He who blasphemes the name of the Lord shall be put to death; all the congregation shall stone him; the sojourner as well as the native, when he blasphemes the Name, shall be put to death. He who kills a man shall be put to death. He who kills a beast shall make it good, life for life. When a man causes a disfigurement in his neighbour, as he has done it shall be done to him, fracture for fracture, eye for eye, tooth for tooth; as he has disfigured a man, he shall be disfigured. He who kills a beast shall make it good; and he who kills a man shall be put to death. You shall have one law for the sojourner and for the native; for I am the Lord your God." So Moses spoke to the people of Israel; and they brought him who had cursed out of the camp, and stoned him with stones. Thus the people of Israel did as the Lord commanded Moses.

In the way that Leviticus tells the story, God's laws were revealed to Moses by trial and error, so to speak. The issue raised here is of one particular individual's misdemeanours, which set Moses seeking the mind of God about what to do with him. The decision then became a precedent for use in later years. That is what today we call "case-law".

The man in this story was not a true member of the Covenant People, being a part-Egyptian. He evidently acted in a deliberately provocative manner, "going about among the people of Israel" stirring up trouble. Whatever the trouble was, he was exciting some Israelites to be disloyal to the Lord. The Name of God, we know from Exod. 3:14, was "I AM", that is to say, the living and eternal God—"This is my Name for ever" (Exod. 3:15). But there is more to the issue than that. This word meaning "I AM", as we have noted earlier, may equally well be rendered from the Hebrew by "I will be with you" (Exod. 3:12).

The greatness of the living and eternal God is far beyond mere man's philosophical ideas about the divine. For God expresses his greatness in the opposite way from what we imagine (as Paul says in 1 Cor. 1). He does so by his humility, his loving condescension, his emptying himself by becoming one partner in a Covenant he has offered to maintain with a sinful and stupid people. This "withness" of God with his people is thus actually his Name. For in those days a name was an actual picture or description of its owner. (See Gen. 17:5; 32:27–28.) How unlike his mother was this part-Egyptian man! Her "name" was *Shelomith,* which means "woman of peace", even "a woman living in fellowship with God".

Using God's Name as a swear word was as nothing compared with what this man was doing. He was actually trying to destroy the faith of the people of Israel by saying that Yahweh, the Lord, was not like his name. He would therefore be insinuating that the idea of the Covenant was a lot of nonsense, and that it was ridiculous to hold the notion that the Creator God could ever be *with* one nation on earth. We can now understand the heinousness of his offence.

Israel gladly shared the love of her God with any non-Israelite who for any reason at all happened to live in her midst. Thus such "sojourners" (v. 16) were to share in the execution of a man who deliberately worked against the loving purpose of God, which was to use Israel and her friends for the salvation of all mankind. Here, by the way, is the only mention of prison in the Old Testament. It is not used for the punishment of a criminal. It is just to hold him in custody till his trial. You do not punish a man by depriving him of his freedom as a child of God. This man has sinned, not against the law, but against God. So *all* Israel (this of course is a metaphorical way of speaking— a million people cannot stone one man) has to get rid of this devilish influence in its midst, and must not leave the deed to Moses alone. In other words, the execution comes from the law of God, not the law of Moses.

The general principle having now been established, that only

God who gives life can take it away, the chapter goes on to describe particular cases. The part-Egyptian man tried to "kill" God's purpose and plan. So now all killing is shown to be what it is—a horror in the sight of God. So it is that even "part-killing", that is, any destruction of just part of a man, e.g. his eye, must be dealt with utterly seriously. The weight of the legal decision in each case will rest on the conscience of the "sojourner" as well, for he receives all the privileges of God's covenantal love along with his host people, the children of Israel.

MUST WE KEEP THE LAW OF MOSES?

Leviticus 25:1–7

> The Lord said to Moses on Mount Sinai, "Say to the people of Israel, When you come into the land which I give you, the land shall keep a sabbath to the Lord. Six years you shall sow your field, and six years you shall prune your vineyard, and gather in its fruits; but in the seventh year there shall be a sabbath of solemn rest for the land, a sabbath to the Lord; you shall not sow your field or prune your vineyard. What grows of itself in your harvest you shall not reap, and the grapes of your undressed vine you shall not gather; it shall be a year of solemn rest for the land. The sabbath of the land shall provide food for you, for yourself and for your male and female slaves and for your hired servant and the sojourner who lives with you; for your cattle also and for the beasts that are in your land all its yield shall be for food."

This chapter has some very important things to say to us today, once we have disentangled the commands of God made in it from the social setting of a people living three thousand years ago. So we must not dodge the issue by suggesting that "these are ridiculous old laws; they do not apply to us in our modern sophisticated society".

The manner in which this chapter opens, however, helps us to see how we are to interpret these laws today. We read: "The Lord said to Moses on Mount Sinai, 'Say to the people of

Israel, When you come into the land which I will give you . . .'."
So the laws were meant for a future period, when conditions
would be quite different. Israel was also in the "wilderness" of
exile in Babylon six hundred years later. Thus Ezra, and others
thereafter, wisely re-thought and re-applied God's laws once
the people were back in their God-given homeland.

What we should recognize therefore is that it was the *spirit* of
God's commands that was to be observed as changes in Israel's
social life kept taking place. There was still another great
change coming in Christ. But the *spirit* of God's laws stood
unchanged. The reason: God is the same yesterday, today and
for ever.

Let us take, for example, the days of the great eighth century
prophets, Amos, Hosea, Micah and Isaiah. Throughout that
century Israel was settled on her own land, the majority of the
people being small farmers or vineyard owners. We see from
Isa. 5:8 that some more prosperous farmers (the ancient
equivalent of the Russian *kulak*?) had at that time become
greedy and were forcibly buying up their neighbour's proper-
ties. The point made here in Leviticus is that such farmers should
exhibit quite a different attitude to the land. For they ought
never to suppose that they could *buy* land, and so make it
belong to them. "The land is mine", says God, "for you are
strangers and sojourners *with* me" (v. 23). Farmers have their
farms on loan only, so to speak, on loan from God. What this
means is that God actually shares *his* land with us, and we are to
use it for his glory, not just for our gain. Farmers too are people
on pilgrimage to the "Promised Land".

So the land of Israel belonged to God. In consequence, Israel
dare not exhaust its resources, or turn it into a dust-bowl, or
exploit it, or use it up so that it turned into a treeless desert.
They were to regard the land with reverence. After all, the land
is no less than Mother Earth, as Gen. 2:7 tells us in picture
theological form—and the people of Israel had already been
told to honour their father and *mother*! That commandment
continues: "that your days may be long in the *land* which the
Lord your God gives you" (Exod. 20:12). Here then, the 4th

Commandment is joined with the 5th Commandment. The land is to keep the Sabbath just as the people are to keep the Sabbath. The land will always provide plenty of food for all. But you are to see it as a live thing which needs rest just as man does.

What then about today? Today we do not need to let land lie fallow in order to recover its potential. The rotation of crops can achieve this instead. We might, however, formulate the command of God in a new way: "Thou shalt not use DDT or napalm on the land, but rather use balanced fertilizers along with nature's own manures"—or something like that!

PROCLAIM LIBERTY TO THE CAPTIVES

Leviticus 25:8–24

"And you shall count seven weeks of years, seven times seven years, so that the time of the seven weeks of years shall be to you forty-nine years. Then you shall send abroad the loud trumpet on the tenth day of the seventh month; on the day of atonement you shall send abroad the trumpet throughout all your land. And you shall hallow the fiftieth year, and proclaim liberty throughout the land to all its inhabitants; it shall be a jubilee for you, when each of you shall return to his property and each of you shall return to his family. A jubilee shall that fiftieth year be to you; in it you shall neither sow, nor reap what grows of itself, nor gather the grapes from the undressed vines. For it is a jubilee; it shall be holy to you; you shall eat what it yields out of the field.

"In this year of jubilee each of you shall return to his property. And if you sell to your neighbour or buy from your neighbour, you shall not wrong one another. According to the number of years after the jubilee, you shall buy from your neighbour, and according to the number of years for crops he shall sell to you. If the years are many you shall increase the price, and if the years are few you shall diminish the price, for it is the number of the crops that he is selling to you. You shall not wrong one another, but you shall fear your God; for I am the Lord your God.

"Therefore you shall do my statutes, and keep my ordinances and perform them; so you will dwell in the land securely. The land will yield its fruit, and you will eat your fill, and dwell in it securely. And if you say, 'What shall we eat in the seventh year, if we may now sow or gather in our crop?' I will command my blessing upon you in the sixth year, so that it will bring forth fruit for three years. When you sow in the eighth year, you will be eating old produce; until the ninth year, when its produce comes in, you shall eat the old. The land shall not be sold in perpetuity, for the land is mine; for you are strangers and sojourners with me. And in all the country you possess, you shall grant a redemption of the land."

Again, the spirit of the command given here to "hold jubilee" must still stand. We should realize that the basic reason for God's gift of the Sabbath was in the first place a humanitarian one. We have seen that it was the one day in the week when a man dare not be compelled to work. *By law* an Israelite could claim his rest day. But then, God's universe is one. In the biblical view, you cannot separate man from his world, his environment. Man is even part of the soil, and his body will return to it when he dies. Seven is the holy number. The figures seven times seven thus represent the ultimate in holiness. So the forty-ninth year is to be followed by a complete Sabbath for all nature to rejoice in. It is to be a "jubilee" year. The word comes from the Hebrew for a ram's horn. This was used as a trumpet to tell everyone that a joyous festival was about to begin.

. The emphasis we find here is on three things. (1) Liberty for all (v. 10), based upon the fact that God had given Israel liberty from Pharaoh's cruel oppression. (2) Complete relaxation offered to everyone so that families might be reunited in joy and contentment, for God loves family life. (A man could even reclaim his ancestral property at this Jubilee if he had been forced, though misfortune or debt, to alienate it. We wonder what those farmers at Isa. 5:8 thought of that!) (3) Freedom for all growing things to recover their natural cycle of life. (Note the fascinating possibility of the renewal of Nature bound up with the renewal of man through the forgiveness that God offers him at the Day of Atonement.)

Incidentally, since the theology of the New Testament cannot be *different* from the theology of the Old Testament, but is its *fulfilment,* we ought to look carefully at this passage. For there are some Christians who declare that only when *individual* men and women have been "born again" can the power of the Gospel get through to the various social issues suggested here. But Leviticus raises two objections to such a theory.

(1) It is the family that first of all knows and experiences the power of God's atoning love, "the love that sets us free with the freedom of Christ"; the individual shares in it ideally only as a member of the family.

(2) The freedom of the Gospel is meant to apply to the whole of man's social and working life (witnessed to by the Sabbath), and not to his individual "soul" alone. Man is not separable from the land which the Lord has lent to him to use in his journey from the cradle to the grave.

The idea of repossessing one's ancestral property, mentioned above, is now developed. First (v. 14), the buying and selling must be done fairly and justly, depending on how long the new owner had enjoyed its use. Why should the transaction be just? The answer comes in two sentences: (a) "You shall fear your God", and (b) "For I am the Lord your God". If only these two sentences could be inserted into all our transactions today! For it is only too easy for developers and trust companies and even private individuals, because of their muscle, to "wrong one another" (v. 14).

Leviticus is concerned with practical measures that could fit in with Isaiah's, or even with Ezra's, day; but Jesus was to present to the world the essence of our passage for all time in the Sermon on the Mount (see Matt. 6:25–33).

PROPERTY DEALS

Leviticus 25:25–38

"If your brother becomes poor, and sells part of his property, then his next of kin shall come and redeem what his brother has sold. If a man has no one to redeem it, and then himself becomes prosperous and finds sufficient means to redeem it, let him reckon the years since he sold it and pay back the overpayment to the man to whom he sold it; and he shall return to his property. But if he has not sufficient means to get it back for himself, then what he sold shall remain in the hand of him who bought it until the year of jubilee; in the jubilee it shall be released, and he shall return to his property.

"If a man sells a dwelling house in a walled city, he may redeem it within a whole year after its sale; for a full year he shall have the right of redemption. If it is not redeemed within a full year, then the house that is in the walled city shall be made sure in perpetuity to him who bought it, throughout his generations; it shall not be released in the jubilee. But the houses of the villages which have no wall around them shall be reckoned with the fields of the country; they may be redeemed, and they shall be released in the jubilee. Nevertheless the cities of the Levites, the houses in the cities of their possession, the Levites may redeem at any time. And if one of the Levites does not exercise his right of redemption, then the house that was sold in a city of their possession shall be released in the jubilee; for the houses in the cities of the Levites are their possession among the people of Israel. But the fields of common land belonging to their cities may not be sold; for that is their perpetual possession.

"And if your brother becomes poor, and cannot maintain himself with you, you shall maintain him; as a stranger and a sojourner he shall live with you. Take no interest from him or increase, but fear your God; that your brother may live beside you. You shall not lend him your money at interest, nor give him your food for profit. I am the Lord your God, who brought you forth out of the land of Egypt to give you the land of Canaan, and to be your God."

Now we deal with the two varieties of life known to Israel after Solomon's day—country and town. Verses 25–28 are about the handling of land in the country, and verse 29 onwards about selling property in the city, including the homes of the Levites. By the end of the Old Testament period the Levites had become ministers of the sanctuary but were subordinate to the priesthood proper (see Ezek. 44:10–14). The emphasis in both cases is (1) upon a just price being paid, and (2) that alienation of a man's property should not be permanent. To use modern terms, the Levite received the free use of a manse or vicarage as part of his stipend, as well as what he received in kind in the form of gifts (Deut. 18:1–5). Since he held his residence in trust from God, Israel had to regard his home also as holy. Being in trust, his home could thus never be alienated. As we say today: "Banks and churches never sell". This meant that if he were "called" from being a village priest to serve on the staff of the Temple in Jerusalem, then there was to be a home there in the city waiting for him and his family to use (Deut. 18:6–8).

People come before property, a reality that the laws of few countries admit today. The people of Israel had known what it means to be poor, hungry and homeless. God had rescued them from that state and had given them their homes, food and clothing. None of them therefore could say: "Look! I did it all myself!" or "We are self-made men!" Because of that, if any Israelite should meet with bad luck and not be able to feed his family, then any relative of his from the large extended family to which he belonged must come to his aid. If he needed money, they must lend it to him, and not take any interest on it. The fate of your brother is more important than merely making money.

The point is that money is not a commodity in its own right. Money is only a means whereby you may feed and clothe your family and show your compassion for the needy and the unfortunate. Our brother is to repay us, not with interest, but with grateful work done. Compassion for him is actually mentioned all of three times, at verses 25, 39, and 47. On the other hand, usury destroys compassion in both the lender and the borrower.

In the Pacific Islands, which are largely deeply Christian in their day-to-day living, no individual would dream of withholding financial aid from any member of the family who might be in trouble. Paying for a student to travel and study at a university overseas is regarded as a natural call upon the finances of the whole family. If the young man gets into trouble of any kind when away, he knows he can fall back on the family still to bail him out.

To help a needy man, you should give him a job. If you do that then you treat him as an employee and not as a slave. Moreover, the rule about freedom for all in the year of jubilee will apply to him and to his family, just as it does to everyone else. God has treated you kindly; you must treat your employees likewise.

OWNING SLAVES

Leviticus 25:39–26:2

"And if your brother becomes poor beside you, and sells himself to you, you shall not make him serve as a slave: he shall be with you as a hired servant and as a sojourner. He shall serve with you until the year of the jubilee; then he shall go out from you, he and his children with him, and go back to his own family, and return to the possession of his fathers. For they are my servants, whom I brought forth out of the land of Egypt; they shall not be sold as slaves. You shall not rule over him with harshness, but shall fear your God. As for your male and female slaves whom you may have: you may buy male and female slaves from among the nations that are round about you. You may also buy from among the strangers who sojourn with you and their families that are with you, who have been born in your land; and they may be your property. You may bequeath them to your sons after you, to inherit as a possession for ever; you may make slaves of them, but over your brethren the people of Israel you shall not rule, one over another, with harshness.

"If a stranger or sojourner with you becomes rich, and your brother beside him becomes poor and sells himself to the stranger or sojourner with you, or to a member of the stranger's family, then after he is sold he may be redeemed; one of his brothers may redeem him, or his uncle, or his cousin may redeem him, or a near kinsman belonging to his family may redeem him; or if he grows rich he may redeem himself. He shall reckon with him who bought him from the year when he sold himself to him until the year of jubilee, and the price of his release shall be according to the number of years; the time he was with his owner shall be rated as the time of a hired servant. If there are still many years, according to them he shall refund out of the price paid for him the price for his redemption. If there remain but a few years until the year of jubilee, he shall make a reckoning with him; according to the years of service due from him he shall refund the money for his redemption. As a servant hired year by year shall he be with him; he shall not rule with harshness over him in your sight. And if he is not redeemed by these means, then he shall be released in the year of jubilee, he and his children with him. For to me the people of Israel are servants, they are my servants whom I brought forth out of the land of Egypt: I am the Lord your God.

"You shall make for yourselves no idols and erect no graven image or pillar, and you shall not set up a figured stone in your land, to bow down to them; for I am the Lord your God. You shall keep my sabbaths and reverence my sanctuary: I am the Lord."

In the days before the invention of industrial machinery, no social system could possibly have carried on without the use of slaves. In the first place Israel was to be allowed to employ only foreigners as slaves. These might be passed on to a man's son in his will. Slavery, therefore, was not evil in itself; it was the possible harshness and cruelty that could be evil. This was illustrated in the way that Israel had already suffered in Egypt.

A Hebrew man could be "redeemed" out of his position of slavery, if he had been unlucky enough in the first place to fall into the hands of a foreigner. "Foreigner" here describes a merchant who comes by with his caravans and sells his wares. Anyone who could afford to do so should "redeem" him. The man might even pay for his manumission himself by saving hard. However, the transaction must be concluded at a just price. There is to be no taking advantage of a foreigner just because he is a foreigner. The word "redeemed" is the same word as that used of God's action when he "redeemed" his servants, the people of Israel, and brought them forth out of the land of Egypt. And so this seemingly rather antiquated passage is actually a piece of theological writing, explaining to us today that God is the God who redeems his children from slavery, industrial, political or social, or even slavery to one's passions and sins, into the freedom of fellowship that is enjoyed within the forgiven community.

At first glance the command in 26:1–2 to erect no graven images or to worship no idols also seems strangely irrelevant to us. We are not tempted to do so today. The mood of the modern world is to believe either in one God or in none. Yet this Word from God stands today as truly as ever.

Israel never fully occupied the Holy Land. We have noted before that many of the indigenous inhabitants remained on in Palestine, living amongst their Israelite conquerors. King David's bodyguard, for example, was composed of foreigners: they were known as Pelethites and Cherethites. The Jebusites were the original inhabitants of Jerusalem. The general name for the native peoples as a whole was Canaanites, as we learn from Judg. 1:27–36. Archaeological research has now provided us with much information on the religions of these various peoples. In a word, all had created their various gods in their own image. Some even learned to accept a god on loan from another nation. Others had their gods imposed on them by a conquering king.

Some of these gods quarrelled amongst themselves. (This is because men quarrel amongst themselves.) Some even fought one another to the death (as men do also). We see some of them vying with one another as they rush madly in pursuit of power, domination, wealth or honour (as men do). Others are full of blood-lust, or of sexual lust, the male gods raping each other's women; in fact treating one another as the objects of the basic egotism of their natures.

Such then were the gods that Israel's Canaanite next-door neighbours actually worshipped in Old Testament times. Our next-door neighbours today also worship the pursuit of power in the community, or bend their whole energies in pursuit of what money can buy, or bow down to acquiring social prestige, or hotly pursue the fruits of a sexually "liberated" society. Just as the power of true love drives out of your mind all false loves, so here, at verse 2, we are given the key to how to resist the subtle blandishments of all these neighbouring gods of ours. It is quite simple. It is to keep the Sabbath as the day which reminds us of the action of the true God in redeeming us from the influence of all these violent and sex-torn gods, and to worship him in his sanctuary. "For *I* am the Lord", not Chemosh, or Baal, or any other idol that reflects the deep sinfulness of the human mind.

SHALOM (Text)

Leviticus 26:3–46

"If you walk in my statutes and observe my commandments and do them, then I will give you your rains in their season, and the land shall yield its increase, and the trees of the field shall yield their fruit. And your threshing shall last to the time of vintage, and the vintage shall last to the time for sowing; and you shall eat your bread to the full, and dwell in your land securely. And I will give peace in the land, and you shall lie down and none shall make you afraid; and I will remove evil beasts from the land, and the sword shall not go through your land. And you shall chase your enemies, and they shall fall before you by the sword. Five of you shall chase a hundred, and a hundred of you shall chase ten thousand; and your enemies shall fall before you by the sword. And I will have regard for you and make you fruitful and multiply you, and will confirm my covenant with you. And you shall eat old store long kept, and you shall clear out the old to make way for the new. And I will make my abode among you, and my soul shall not abhor you. And I will walk among you, and will be your God, and you shall be my people. I am the Lord your God, who brought you forth out of the land of Egypt, that you should not be their slaves; and I have broken the bars of your yoke and made you walk erect.

"But if you will not hearken to me, and will not do all these commandments, if you spurn my statutes, and if your soul abhors my ordinances, so that you will not do all my commandments, but break my covenant, I will do this to you: I will appoint over you sudden terror, consumption and fever that waste the eyes and cause life to pine away. And you shall sow your seed in vain, for your enemies shall eat it; I will set my face against you, and you shall be smitten before your enemies; those who hate you shall rule over you, and you shall flee when none pursues you. And if in spite of this you will not hearken to me, then I will chastise you again sevenfold for your sins, and I will break the pride of your power, and I will make your heavens like iron and your earth like brass; and your strength shall be spent in vain, for your land shall not yield its increase, and the trees of the land shall not yield their fruit.

"Then if you walk contrary to me, and will not hearken to me, I will bring more plagues upon you, sevenfold as many as your sins. And I will let loose the wild beasts among you, which shall rob you of your children, and destroy your cattle, and make you few in number, so that your ways shall become desolate.

"And if by this discipline you are not turned to me, but walk contrary to me, then I also will walk contrary to you, and I myself will smite you sevenfold for your sins. And I will bring a sword upon you, that shall execute vengeance for the covenant; and if you gather within your cities I will send pestilence among you, and you shall be delivered into the hand of the enemy. When I break your staff of bread, ten women shall bake your bread in one oven, and shall deliver your bread again by weight; and you shall eat, and not be satisfied.

"And if in spite of this you will not hearken to me, but walk contrary to me, then I will walk contrary to you in fury, and chastise you myself sevenfold for your sins. You shall eat the flesh of your sons, and you shall eat the flesh of your daughters. And I will destroy your high places, and cut down your incense altars, and cast your dead bodies upon the dead bodies of your idols; and my soul will abhor you. And I will lay your cities waste, and will make your sanctuaries desolate, and I will not smell your pleasing odours. And I will devastate the land, so that your enemies who settle in it shall be astonished at it. And I will scatter you among the nations, and I will unsheathe the sword after you; and your land shall be a desolation, and your cities shall be a waste.

"Then the land shall enjoy its sabbaths as long as it lies desolate, while you are in your enemies' land; then the land shall rest, and enjoy its sabbaths. As long as it lies desolate it shall have rest, the rest which it had not in your sabbaths when you dwelt upon it. And as for those of you that are left, I will send faintness into their hearts in the lands of their enemies; the sound of a driven leaf shall put them to flight, and they shall flee as one flees from the sword, and they shall fall when none pursues. They shall stumble over one another, as if to escape a sword, though none pursues; and you shall have no power to stand before your enemies. And you shall perish among the nations, and the land of your enemies shall eat you up. And those of you that are left shall pine away in your enemies' lands because of their iniquity; and also because of the iniquities of their fathers they shall pine away like them.

"But if they confess their iniquity and the iniquity of their fathers in their treachery which they committed against me, and also in walking contrary to me, so that I walked contrary to them and brought them into the land of their enemies; if then their uncircumcised heart is humbled and they make amends for their iniquity; then I will remember my covenant with Jacob, and I will remember my covenant with Isaac and my covenant with Abraham, and I will remember the land. But the land shall be left by them, and enjoy its sabbaths while it lies desolate without them; and they shall make amends for their inquity, because they spurned my ordinances, and their soul abhorred my statutes. Yet for all that, when they are in the land of their enemies, I will not spurn them, neither will I abhor them so as to destroy them utterly and break my covenant with them; for I am the Lord their God; but I will for their sake remember the covenant with their forefathers, whom I brought forth out of the land of Egypt in the sight of the nations, that I might be their God: I am the Lord."

These are the statutes and ordinances and laws which the Lord made between him and the people of Israel on Mount Sinai by Moses.

SHALOM (Commentary)

Leviticus 26:3–46 (*cont'd*)

We have the conviction expressed here once again that man is all bound up with Nature. If a man would only live in harmony with God, then Nature too would be in harmony with man. This is in accord with the great vision of Isaiah at Isa. 11:1–9; but there we see that this universal harmony will come about only after God has acted in a new way through the messianic son of David still to come. "I will give you peace in the *land*" (v. 6) and not just "in your heart", "peace" being the Hebrew word *shalom* that everyone knows, and which includes within it the deep idea of harmony. And this harmony will then make itself apparent in politics, international relations, the health of the home, and even the safety of babies.

God's care for his people, then, would cover the lean years by his granting extra fat years, as in the story of Joseph in Egypt (Gen. 41). This harmony would be grounded in a blessed relationship between the Covenant God and his Covenant People (v. 9, v. 11–12). And so this passage gives us a picture of the meaning of the word "salvation" as the Old Testament uses it. Today when people talk of transcendence, meaning "God out there", they miss what this passage is saying. It is that while God is indeed *out there,* he is also *here.* "I will make my abode with you, and I will walk among you, and will be your God and you shall be my people." What a difference that makes when we feel tempted to worship our modern idols! Moreover, it is here and now that the promise is meant for (vv. 9–11). The *present* experience of fulness of life is really the first-fruits of the *shalom,* peace, harmony, fulness of life, that is *there* all the time in the life beyond.

Emphasis is laid once again upon God's act of "prevenient grace", that is, his redemption of his people before they could ever help themselves. Israel celebrated this fact by circumcizing each new baby boy born into the Covenant people. Once the Church, with Paul's help in Rom. 9–11, had thought through the fact that it was not a new institution in the world, but was rooted in Abraham just as much as the Jewish people were, it too did the same. Only it made use of baptism. This for two reasons: firstly, baptism was the rite employed when a gentile joined himself to the Jewish community in the first century A.D. Secondly, since we are now all one in Jesus Christ, Jew and gentile, male and female, baptism was used for the baby girl too, so that she could claim the same heritage as her little brother.

God had now created a race of free men and women, proudly walking erect (v. 13). They could do so because they could rejoice in a God who had done all these mighty deeds *for* them. What a difference there is, then, between God's People Israel, freemen all, and their neighbours who are still slaves to their sensual passions, lust for power, or greed to obtain what money can buy.

So great is this difference that those Israelites who do not realize the meaning of grace naturally place themselves under a terrible judgment. Fancy spurning the joy of freedom and the opportunity to walk erect with the living God, choosing instead slavery to gods created by one's own imagination! Judgment *must* follow. This is brought home to us in vivid language (like that used by Jesus in Matt. 15, and in Matt. 23–24). God's judgment touches a man at all points of his life, since the true fellowship with God which he now "abhors" (v. 15) is also a total one that covers all aspects of human life. This rejection of grace makes a man afraid of death. It turns the ordered civilization of man back into the chaos pictured in Gen. 1:2. And so the judgment is described as no less than hell—hell on earth. But then, what men do on earth is of eternal significance, and so hell must be reality in eternity also. How clearly this is brought out by Jesus in his repeated emphasis upon the Day of Judgment (Matt. 5:22; 10:15; 12:36)!

THE FIRST DAY OF JUDGMENT

Leviticus 26:3–46 (*cont'd*)

There was a historical period when God's judgment upon apostasy was made plain for all to see. We read of it in the story of revelation in the Bible. That period began in the year 587 B.C. when Nebuchadnezzar king of Babylon totally destroyed the city of Jerusalem and ravished the land of Judah. Then it was that children perished both by starvation and by the sword, and that old people were whipped into line as they set off in long procession "with a hook through the nose" to trudge with all their worldly possessions on their backs the agonizing seven hundred miles of dusty, rainless track from the Holy Land to the life of daily sweat as labourers in Babylon. But more than that—to a life of separation from the living God. "I will appoint over you sudden terror, consumption and fever that wastes" (v. 16).

And worse still—God's Covenant, spoken of at verse 9,

would seem to have been an illusion. The Temple, the "sanctuary" which Israel was to reverence (v. 2), had become a burnt-out ruin. God's promise to the line of David (2 Sam. 7; 12–16) must have been a mere myth. The Holy Land was no longer holy; it had been desecrated, its fruit trees destroyed, its life-giving wells stopped up. Jeremiah had declared that this desolation (v. 34) would last for seventy years (Jer. 25: 8–11), "because you have not obeyed my words". The number seventy being ten times the blessed number seven, the judgment was regarded as the reverse of the promise of God's blessing upon his people if they had remained faithful to his covenantal plan for them. The Jubilee Sabbath of joy and peace had become its obverse—it was now a *Jubilee of desolation.* The land would "enjoy" (Oh, the irony of that word!) its seventy-year-long Sabbath, and would have rest indeed—the rest and peace of the cemetery.

I would make three points here:

(1) The greatest compliment God can pay man, says a theologian, is to confront him with the reality of hell.

(2) This chapter is the answer to the question people have asked from time immemorial: "If God is love, why does he allow things like this to happen? Clearly he cannot be all-loving and all-powerful at the same time."

(3) To cover all aspects of the judgment the writer is careful to say that even those citizens of Jerusalem who were not dragged off into exile, but stayed in comparative peace in the ruins of Jerusalem, had to meet with the judgment of God (v. 36–39). There is no escaping the judgment of the Hound of Heaven.

THE CONTINUING DAY OF JUDGMENT

Whose fate is pronounced here in this terrible language? That of the Pelethites, the Hittites, the Babylonians? Surely not. The Old Testament never hesitates to affirm that all men are under the judgment of God (see Amos 1–2). On the other hand, Israel has received a special blessing because God has elected her in love. As Amos put it bluntly: "You only have I known, (chosen, elected, loved) of all the families of the earth" (Amos 3:2). Now, a blessing is a word spoken with power to do what it is uttered to do. A blessing coming out of the mouth of God is like an arrow he has shot that nothing in heaven or earth can prevent from flying till it reaches its target. Thus nothing can deflect the flight of God's arrow of love, not even death and hell itself. However, that is not the end of Amos's pronouncement. He goes on: "therefore I will punish you, says the Lord."

Israel must learn that if she is specially blessed, then she is in danger of being specially damned. It would seem that Israel must learn by the very nature of things that her "cup of blessing" must become her "cup of damnation" (Jer. 25:15; 1 Cor. 11:29). The manna in the desert, God's gift of food to strengthen his chosen people, becomes a maggoty mess if it is rejected and misused. Israel had been chosen to be God's instrument in his plan to bring in the day when every knee should bow to him (Isa. 45:23). In parallel with this, yet of course more than a mere parallel, we discover the continuing revelation of God's intention when we come to New Testament times. For the Church, the People of the New Covenant, has now been chosen to be the instrument in God's plan that every knee should bow to him, and every tongue should give him (Christ) praise (Rom. 14:11). If therefore the chosen instrument of that universal plan should itself be the means of frustrating the realization of that plan, then the People of God must surely bear a curse beyond anything that natural man, as he clings to the various religions and ideologies of the world, will ever have to suffer. Since this fact is little understood by those who call themselves either Jews or Christians, such astonishing blindness is surely the penalty for the egotism that lurks in the heart even of the professed believer. "I will break the pride of your power" (v. 19) says God here. We recall that the Church has always declared that pride is the worst of the seven deadly sins.

The word "remember" is prominent here. How often do we read that God is always ready to *remember* Israel. But Israel persistently *forgets* Yahweh, not in a whimsical way like when I forget to bring home a pound of sausages. The word here means to forget with the *will*, to do so with deliberation, so that one develops a kind of amnesia about God and his love. Paul understood all this well. In 1 Cor. 10 he declares that the stories in the *Torah* were written as a warning for us *in the Christian era!*

GOD'S PRESENCE IS THE BLESSING

Leviticus 26:3–46 (*cont'd*)

But the arrow that God has shot is always the same arrow. This is because God himself does not change. And so his spoken Word stands for ever. God does not recall his arrow, though he may change his plan. We find this spoken of in Genesis under the term "repent" (e.g. Gen. 6:6, AV). That of course has nothing to do with what the word means in modern English. To recall his arrow would be magic, and God does not deal in magic. The Word spoken as a blessing must necessarily remain a blessing. Even when it becomes a Word of judgment it will still continue to re-create Israel's life, and despite Israel's effrontery and rebellious spirit what happens is, "then I will remember my covenant" (v. 42), the Covenant he has made, both with the patriarchs and with the *land*. This last phrase develops out of what is said at verse 32.

The content of a blessing from God is this, that out of evil God creates good. So here, out of Israel's effrontery, God recreates humility and awareness of sin. Even an "uncircumcised heart", that is to say, one that belongs to the rebellious individual who has cut himself off from those who belong in God's Covenant, the mark of which is circumcision, can be humbled in this way. So the curse upon both Israel and the land is actually God's blessing in disguise; for it is the Word of God which, as an arrow in flight, no demons from hell can hope to avert from the target to which it is flying. When God's Word is uttered, it is like the rain which comes down from heaven (Isa. 55:10–11). Nothing can stop the rain from falling, for it is coming down with the one purpose in view of watering the ground so that man might have food to eat.

What a profundity of theology we have met with in this one chapter alone! Yet it is but one of the many quarries searched by St. Paul from which he hewed the theology that we meet with in his Letter to the Romans. Paul did not invent his theology of grace, of the Cross, of forgiveness, of the power of the Word merely out of the air. So many aspects of the *meaning* of Christ given to us by New Testament thinkers in their writings have been set down here already in the Old Testament where we are able to witness God revealing himself in a love to Israel that goes beyond even death and hell. Indeed, the love of this Covenanting God of ours is describable only in the words of our hymn: "O love that wilt not let me go". Why should God be like that? "For I am God, and not man" (Hos. 11:9).

So ends at 26:46 the Holiness Code that began with chapter 17, not with a climactic series of legal demands, but with one of the greatest pieces of theological writing of all time.

PAYING ONE'S DUES

Leviticus 27:1–34

The Lord said to Moses, "Say to the people of Israel, When a man makes a special vow of persons to the Lord at your valuation, then your valuation of a male from twenty years old up to sixty years old shall be fifty shekels of silver, according to the shekel of the sanctuary. If the person is a female, your valuation shall be thirty shekels. If the person is from five years old up to twenty years old, your valuation shall be for a male twenty shekels, and for a female ten shekels. If the person is from a month old up to five years old, your valuation shall be for a male five shekels of silver, and for a female your valuation shall be three shekels of silver. And if the person is sixty years old and upward, then your valuation for a male shall be fifteen shekels, and for a female ten shekels. And if a man is too poor to pay your valuation, then he shall bring the person before the priest, and the priest shall value him; according to the ability of him who vowed the priest shall value him.

"If it is an animal such as men offer as an offering to the Lord, all of such that any man gives to the Lord is holy. He shall not substitute anything for it or exchange it, a good for a bad, or a bad for a good; and if he makes any exchange of beast for beast, then both it and that for which it is exchanged shall be holy. And if it is an unclean animal such as is not offered as an offering to the Lord, then the man shall bring the animal before the priest, and the priest shall value it as either good or bad; as you, the priest, value it, so it shall be. But if he wishes to redeem it, he shall add a fifth to the valuation.

"When a man dedicates his house to be holy to the Lord, the priest shall value it as either good or bad; as the priest values it, so it shall stand. And if he who dedicates it wishes to redeem his house, he shall add a fifth of the valuation in money to it, and it shall be his.

"If a man dedicates to the Lord part of the land which is his by inheritance, then your valuation shall be according to the seed for it; a sowing of a homer of barley shall be valued at fifty shekels of silver. If he dedicates his field from the year of jubilee, it shall stand at your full valuation; but if he dedicates his field after the jubilee, then the priest shall compute the money-value for it according to the years that remain until the year of jubilee, and a deduction shall be made from your valuation. And if he who dedicates the field wishes to redeem it, then he shall add a fifth of the valuation in money to it, and it shall remain his. But if he does not wish to redeem the field, or if he has sold the field to another man, it shall not be redeemed any more; but the field, when it is released in the jubilee, shall be holy to the Lord, as a field that has been devoted; the priest shall be in possession of it. If he dedicates to the Lord a field which he has bought, which is not a part of his possession by inheritance, then the priest shall compute the valuation for it up to the year of jubilee, and the man shall give the amount of the valuation on that day as a holy thing to the Lord. In the year of jubilee the field shall return to him from whom it was bought, to whom the land belongs as a possession by inheritance. Every valuation shall be according to the shekel of the sanctuary: twenty gerahs shall make a shekel.

"But a firstling of animals, which as a firstling belongs to the Lord, no man may dedicate; whether ox or sheep, it is the Lord's. And if it is an unclean animal, then he shall buy it back at your valuation, and add a fifth to it; or, if it is not redeemed, it shall be sold at your valuation.

"But no devoted thing that a man devotes to the Lord, of anything that he has, whether of man or beast, or of his inherited field, shall be sold or redeemed; every devoted thing is most holy to the Lord. No one devoted, who is to be utterly destroyed from among men, shall be ransomed; he shall be put to death.

"All the tithe of the land, whether of the seed of the land or of the fruit of the trees, is the Lord's; it is holy to the Lord. If a man wishes to redeem any of his tithe, he shall add a fifth to it. And all the tithe of herds and flocks, every tenth animal of all that pass under the herdsman's staff, shall be holy to the Lord. A man shall not inquire whether it is good or bad, neither shall he exchange it; and if he exchanges it, then both it and that for which it is exchanged shall be holy; it shall not be redeemed."

These are the commandments which the Lord commanded Moses for the people of Israel on Mount Sinai.

This last chapter is a late addition to the whole book. It deals with a situation that probably didn't arise until the Temple had been rebuilt and rededicated in 515 B.C. after the return from exile.

Today we talk of making a commitment to God. Here we have rather the idea of paying God a vow, and so of promising to give so much towards the cost of the upkeep of the Temple sacrifices. This code here offers a sliding scale as a suggestion for use by both young and old. But a promise like the one described here was absolutely binding, and simply had to be kept, as we see if we look at Num. 30:2. Since a man daren't promise to give more than he could afford, he got a priest to assess how much he should vow (v. 8). This promise was a kind of voluntary income tax for the upkeep of the Temple made on an assessment of income, age, and status in the community.

A man could vow an animal (v. 9) to be sacrificed at the altar in place of money. Of course the beast had to be a valuable one, "without blemish". But if it were the wrong kind of animal, then the priest could demand the financial value of the beast instead of the beast itself. Then, if the offerer decided to take the beast back, he would have to pay an extra 20% on its value.

The same valuation goes if a man vows his house (v. 14) to God, or part of his land (v. 16). Since all lands revert to their original owner at Jubilee year, the amount paid on the land depended on how far away the Jubilee year was. A double sale did not count, however (v. 20–21). In such a case the piece of land in question reverted to the Temple.

It was impossible however to do this kind of things with the first-born of any animal (v. 26). For of course the first-born already belonged to the Lord (Exod. 13:2,12). This was why all Israel belonged to God, for all Israel was God's first-born son (Exod. 4:22).

THE MEANING OF THIS CHAPTER

Leviticus 27:1–34 (*cont'd*)

The theology behind these ideas, we find, grows and expands over the years throughout the Old Testament period.

(1) The blessing of God to the world was meant to work through Israel, the first-born son, to reach all God's other sons. The other nations were thereupon blessed *in* Israel. This happens because God has acted first in bringing his saving love to earth. This act of God is what theologians call his "prevenient grace". God chose, selected, or if you like, elected Abraham, the "father" of the people of Israel (Gen. 12:1). Then he *blessed* Abraham. Whereupon Abraham's descendants were to be the instrument of God's blessing to "all the families of the earth". In the same way, Paul sees Jesus to be "the first-born among many brethren" (Rom. 8:29). And thus, next in sequence, as Paul declares (1 Cor. 15:20), "Christ has been raised from the dead, the first-fruits of those who have fallen asleep." What we read here in Leviticus, therefore, is the basic idea from which the whole theology of the first-fruits arises.

(2) The question how much a person ought to pay to God, either in cash or in kind, in order to avoid retribution for his sins, raises several issues:

(a) A man can do so only temporarily and only as suited the situation to be found in the century B.C. in which he lived. As Jesus put it later, "For your hardness of heart he gave you this commandment" (this was about the meaning of marriage, not actually the question before us). What Jesus meant was that the Law was intended to be "valid" only temporarily, only until the kingdom of God dawned, as it was doing even then in himself.

(b) The question of a man's value, however, has now been raised. What Jesus wants us to think about is how to answer the question of a man's *real* value. "Are you not of more value than the birds of the air?" (Matt. 6:26)

(c) Again, as we have seen repeatedly, in those old days of the Law certain aspects of life undoubtedly belonged to God. They were thus "holy". But all those areas of life were connected with the cult, with Israel's worship, and they had to do with the *place* which God had made holy for himself. But could the all-holy God remain satisfied with only portions of human life being made holy to himself? The prophet Zechariah could not believe that. The last verse of his book (written, of course, even later than this last chapter of Leviticus) looks to the day when the pots and pans in people's kitchens would be just as holy as were the holy vessels in the Temple; and the horses that do the world's work and take men into battle to keep law and order in the world would have (symbolically speaking) the words "Holy to the Lord" inscribed on the bells round their necks.

So then, having read this chapter, let us hear what Paul says. "I appeal to you therefore, brethren, by the mercies of God, to present your bodies as a living sacrifice [not an animal substitute] *holy* and acceptable to God" (Rom. 12:1). The pattern for the meaning of holiness has been here all along in Leviticus!

Finally, what about the sacrifice itself? Let us draw together a few ideas out of Leviticus. Man is a sinner. By grace God has made him conscious that he is a sinner as we read in the previous chapter. In order to be right with the holy God, however, man must first be made holy. This can happen only through sacrifice. Man cannot sacrifice his own self because he is not "without blemish" as a sinner. But a substitute "without blemish" may die on his behalf. This substitute must itself be holy and without blemish. Through the sacrifice of this substitute a man's life can be redeemed, or bought back, or given back to him.

The substitute which is sacrificed must be "devoted" to the Lord, for only then is the substitute "most holy to the Lord" (v. 28). The sacrifice must be totally and utterly destroyed (v. 29). The word here is the Hebrew *cherem*. This term describes what Joshua did to the city of Jericho when he sent it up in smoke to God, *completely and utterly*. So "the devoted thing given to the Lord" (v. 28–29) cannot ransom itself, though it is now the *asham* or guilt offering. So it must be another who now becomes the ransom for the sinner, one who is willing to make the ultimate and absolute commitment for the price of man; and that can happen only if he be willing to be a *cherem,* that is, a total sacrifice. As Paul insists, it is only God himself, uttering his Word which is both blessing and curse at the same time, who can do this thing: and it is just this that God actually does, *in* Christ (2 Cor. 5:19).

Is this last chapter of Leviticus merely a rather dull addition to the long Holiness Code which we have now examined in detail? Indeed it is not. For do we not find here the theological pattern which makes the work of Christ intelligible to the world?

FURTHER READING

COMMENTARIES

M. Noth, *Leviticus: A Commentary* (Old Testament Library) (SCM and Westminster Press, 1962)

J.L. Mays, *Leviticus, Numbers* (The Layman's Bible Commentaries) (SCM and John Knox Press, 1963)

J.R. Porter, *Leviticus* (The Cambridge Bible Commentary on the New English Bible) (Cambridge University Press, 1976)

N.H. Snaith, *Leviticus and Numbers* (The Century Bible, New Edition) (Nelson, 1967)

STUDIES

B.A. Levine, *In the Presence of the Lord: A Study of Cult and some Cultic Terms in Ancient Israel* (Brill, Leiden, 1974)

J. Milgrom, *The ASHAM and the Priestly Doctrine of Repentance* (Brill, Leiden, 1976)

R. de Vaux, *Studies in Old Testament Sacrifice* (University of Wales Press, Cardiff, 1964)